Praise for

Inferno

"Of many noble tries to render Dante's m_____ English, Michael Palma's may well be the noblest of all. In capturing the sense, sound, and spirit of the original, his wonderfully readable translation comes close to perfection. I'm tempted to call it a miracle."

—X. J. Kennedy

"I think highly of Michael Palma's *Inferno*. It is accurate as to sense, fully rhymed, and easy, as a rule, in its movement through the tercets. Readers will find it admirably clear and readable."

—Richard Wilbur

"After a lifetime of reading translations which I always thought I could improve, I find Michael Palma's *Inferno* to be one that I'm having a hard time improving."

—Lawrence Ferlinghetti

"Without ever betraying the literal sense of every line, Palma renders the music of Dante's thinking in a remarkable way. This is a grand accomplishment and a genuine surprise."

—Giuseppe Mazzotta, Yale University

"I believe that Palma's work will become the translation of choice for most readers. Despite the strictures of rhyme, it contains so many strong passages which capture the economy and speed of Dante's original that it stands in a class apart."

—John Ahern, Vassar College

"Palma's apparently effortless mastery of rhyme, his control of syntax, and his skill at pacing and variety are all crucial components of this translation's weight, its authority, and at the same time its deceptive simplicity."

—Rachel Hadas

THE NORTON LIBRARY

Inferno

MICHAEL PALMA is the recipient of the Italo Calvino Award for his translation of *My Name on the Wind: Selected Poems of Diego Valeri* and of the Raiziss/de Palchi Translation Award from the American Academy of American Poets for his translation of *The Man I Pretend to Be: "The Colloquies" and Selected Poems of Guido Gozzano*. Palma has published four collections of verse: *The Egg Shape, Antibodies, A Fortune in Gold,* and *Begin in Gladness,* and an Internet chapbook, *The Ghost of Congress Street,* as well as *Faithful in My Fashion: Essays on the Translation of Poetry*.

THE NORTON LIBRARY

2020–2021

For a complete list of titles in the Norton Library, visit wwnorton.com/norton-library

THE NORTON LIBRARY

Dante Alighieri
Inferno

Translated by
Michael Palma

W. W. NORTON & COMPANY
Independent Publishers Since 1923

W. W. Norton & Company has been independent since its founding in 1923, when William Warder Norton and Mary D. Herter Norton first published lectures delivered at the People's Institute, the adult education division of New York City's Cooper Union. The firm soon expanded its program beyond the Institute, publishing books by celebrated academics from America and abroad. By midcentury, the two major pillars of Norton's publishing program—trade books and college texts—were firmly established. In the 1950s, the Norton family transferred control of the company to its employees, and today—with a staff of five hundred and hundreds of trade, college, and professional titles published each year—W. W. Norton & Company stands as the largest and oldest publishing house owned wholly by its employees.

Editor: Pete Simon
Associate Editor: Katie Pak
Project Editor: Maura Gaughan
Manufacturing by: LSC Communications
Compositor: Westchester Publishing Services
Book design by: Marisa Nakasone
Production Manager: Jeremy Burton

Library of Congress Cataloging-in-Publication Data

Names: Dante Alighieri, 1265–1321, author. | Palma, Michael, 1945–translator.
Title: Inferno / Dante Alighieri ; translated by Michael Palma.
Other titles: Inferno. English | Norton library.
Description: New York : W. W. Norton & Company, 2020.
Series: The Norton library
Identifiers: LCCN 2020016349 | ISBN 9780393427981 (paperback)
Classification: LCC PQ4315.2 .P27 2020 | DDC 851/.1—dc23
LC record available at https://lccn.loc.gov/2020016349

ISBN: 978-0-393-42798-1 (pbk.)

W. W. Norton & Company, Inc., 500 Fifth Avenue, New York, N.Y. 10110
www.wwnorton.com

W. W. Norton & Company Ltd., 15 Carlisle Street, London W1D 3BS

1 2 3 4 5 6 7 8 9 0

Contents

Introduction

One of the places in which Good Friday would have been observed in 1300 was the Italian city of Firenze, or Florence, as it is known in English. Founded in 59 B.C.E. by Julius Caesar, Florence in the medieval era was a powerful political force and bustling financial center that was home to over fifty thousand people, one of whom was a poet and public official in his mid-thirties named Dante Alighieri. We do not know precisely how the real-life Dante Alighieri spent Good Friday in the year 1300; record-keeping of that sort was infinitely less copious and detailed at that time than it is in our own. We do know, however, in extensive and at times horrifying detail, what his fictional alter ego was doing on that occasion: paying a visit—luckily for him, a temporary one—to hell itself.

Dante's *Inferno*, the poetic record of that visit, is one of those books, like *Don Quixote* and *Moby-Dick*, whose broad outlines are known to virtually everyone: as he tells us in the opening lines, Dante strays into a dark wood where he is rescued by the shade of the Roman poet Virgil, who takes him on a guided tour of hell, which is located inside the earth. To Dante, who did not know Greek and thus had no experience of Homer's *Iliad* or *Odyssey*, Virgil's *Aeneid* was the great classical epic. Dante and his educated contemporaries admired the Latin poem for its elevated style and sublimity of purpose, and Virgil was also esteemed in the Middle Ages because of the widespread but mistaken belief that in the fourth of his *Eclogues* he had prophesied the birth of Christ. These reasons are sufficient to suggest the appropriateness of Virgil as Dante's guide through the underworld, but the choice of the Roman poet is even more obvious in light of Book VI of the *Aeneid*, in which the protagonist, Aeneas, is given a tour of the underworld, where, among other experiences, he sees the shades of the wicked in the region called Tartarus. On his own journey, Dante interacts, often quite extensively, with a number of the damned souls that he encounters along the way.

It is also generally known that Dante's conception of hell divides it into a number of levels, or circles. There are nine circles in all, each of which is given over to the punishment of a particular class of sins, and these circles are ranked according to the increasing severity of the offenses in question. In our own time, it is not uncommon to encounter references to some especially egregious behavior as being worthy of this or that one of Dante's circles. Such descriptions are often allusions to the famous device of the *contrapasso*—the word occurs at the end of Canto XXVIII—the fitting of the punishment to the crime. (Each section, or chapter, of the poem is called a *canto*, Italian for "song." Cantos IV through VII each describe one of the first four circles of hell; had Dante continued in this fashion, the poem would be about a third of its present length, but as he goes on, the various locations are described in increasing depth and detail; together the eighth circle—with its ten concentric ditches, or *bolge*—and the ninth take up seventeen cantos, half the entire poem.)

There are also a number of phrases from the text of the *Inferno* that have become part of the general stock of familiar quotations in English, beginning with the very first lines of the poem: "Midway through the journey of our life, I found / myself in a dark wood, for I had strayed / from the straight pathway." Note, in the opening line, the highly significant word "our," which signals from the beginning that the poem's theme will have a universal application, not a merely personal one. Perhaps the single most famous line appears near the beginning of Canto III. It is the conclusion of the inscription over the gate of hell, as rendered two centuries ago by the British clergyman Henry Francis Cary, in one of the first English translations of the work, and the very first to possess genuine literary merit: "All hope abandon, ye who enter here." And just a few lines later comes a passage made famous in English through its inclusion in *The Waste Land* by T. S. Eliot, who acknowledged Dante as his greatest poetic influence and whose own poems abound in echoes of the Italian poet's lines: "I had not thought death had undone so many."

The afterlife of the damned as imagined by Dante is very different from the customary depiction of hell as a place in which all the dead wail incessantly as they are consumed by fierce eternal flames. In English the word *inferno* denotes a conflagration, no doubt because of the association of hell with fire, but the Italian word that Dante chose for the title of his poem comes from a Latin term meaning "lower" (as in *inferior*) and simply indicates hell, without any necessary association with fire. There are many different kinds of punishments in the *Inferno*. Fire is indeed one of them, in Cantos XXVI and XXVII. Its most notable victims are Ulysses (the Odysseus of Homer's *Iliad* and *Odyssey*) and Guido da Montefeltro, a leader of the Ghibellines, one of two factions (the other being the Guelphs) whose rivalry was the major source of conflict in medieval Italy. But the very bottom of hell, at the center of the earth's core, where the worst sinners of all are punished and Satan himself is entrapped, is a region of bitterly cold wind and universal ice.

Many people who have never read the *Inferno* could also tell you that it is the first of three units (the others being the *Purgatorio* and the *Paradiso*), roughly equal in length, that together form the work that Dante called the *Commedia*, or the *Comedy*, but which has been known since the sixteenth century as the *Divine Comedy*. The word *comedy* here does not, as it does nowadays, connote mirth and laughter. In classical terms, it signifies a work written in the low style (as opposed to Virgil's "lofty verses," as Dante describes them several times) that tends toward a happy ending (in this case, the availability of eternal salvation to the protagonist, and to all who truly desire it). Despite differences in style, the *Divine Comedy* is a work of epic length, scope, and depth, like its Virgilian model.

Many people could probably also tell you that the *Comedy* is written in *terza rima*, or "third rhyme," a form created by Dante for this work. *Terza rima* is composed of three-line units called tercets, in each of which the first and third lines rhyme with one another and the second line rhymes with the first and third lines of the following tercet, thus creating components that are simultaneously independent and interlocking. Metrically, it is written in hendecasyllabics, or eleven-syllable lines, in which every other syllable, beginning with the second, is stressed. Since the vast majority of Italian words have an unstressed final syllable, this meter corresponds to the English iambic pentameter, a ten-syllable line in which the accents fall on the even-numbered syllables. In fact, the most famous line of poetry in the English language, from Shakespeare's *Hamlet*, is a hendecasyllabic: "To be or not to be: that is the question."

So, first-time readers of the *Inferno* come to it with a considerable body of assumptions that will be confirmed when they read the text. At the same time, however, they are likely to encounter a number of surprising elements. They are certain to be surprised, if not astonished, by Dante's ranking of the relative grievousness of certain sins. For instance, tyrants and murderers are in the seventh circle. But placed lower, and punished more severely, in the various *bolge* of the eighth circle are soothsayers, hypocrites, and even flatterers. How, we might well ask ourselves, can killing people possibly be a less terrible sin than telling what we would call a little white lie in order to spare someone's feelings? The answer is given in the eleventh canto, in which Virgil explains the system and structure of hell to Dante: sins of appetite and emotion, qualities that we share with animals, are less offensive than those that require intellect, because the latter involve perversion of the faculty of reason, which God has given to humans alone, in order that they may know, love, and serve Him, and thus secure their salvation. Perhaps the clearest and most famous illustration of this hierarchy is the fact that Dante places the adulterous lovers Paolo and Francesca in the second circle, among the least severely punished of the damned.

The Enduring Importance of the *Inferno*

Our pool of culturally informed people who have never read the *Inferno* could probably tell you that, over and above its interest as a literary classic, it is a work of great historical importance and influence. At a time when Latin was still the preferred language for texts of moral import and intellectual seriousness, Dante chose to write the *Comedy* in the vernacular, the "vulgar tongue," the common spoken language of his time and place. As a result of his achievement, his local Tuscan dialect became the standard written language we now know as Italian, and that language has remained remarkably stable in the seven hundred years since Dante wrote his poem. A contemporary Italian speaker can read it with immensely less difficulty than a modern-day English speaker might read an Anglo-Saxon text from the early fourteenth century.

To fully grasp how the *Divine Comedy* was received in its own time, we need a basic understanding of what that time was like. In the millennium since the Edict of Milan in 313 had established tolerance for Christianity in the Roman Empire, the previously persecuted sect had grown and taken hold to the point where the Roman Catholic Church dominated virtually every aspect of life in western Europe (the Protestant Reformation was still more than two hundred years in the future). Life on earth was seen as a prelude to the eternal life that followed after death, and the manner in which one lived while upon the earth determined where, and under what conditions, that eternal existence would be spent. The domination of this religious emphasis extended to learning and the arts as well. Since the majority of people were uneducated and illiterate, the visual and plastic arts of painting, sculpture, and architecture were especially significant as embodiments of the spiritual dimension. Literacy and learning were essentially the province of spiritual and secular authority, and, as we shall see, the line between the authority of the church and the authority of temporal government was growing increasingly blurred.

The *Divine Comedy* was recognized from the beginning as a great achievement and a major work of literature, and commentaries on the text began to appear in the 1320s, not long after Dante's death in September 1321. (During the Renaissance, however, with the emphasis on more humanistic values in place of explicitly didactic ones, its cultural influence waned somewhat.) The number of such texts and the learning displayed in many of them bore testimony to the high regard in which Dante's work was held by his contemporaries and immediate successors. The majority of these commentaries annotated the *Comedy* on a line-by-line basis, providing interpretations of individual passages and supplying background information on persons and events, and on biblical, mythological, and other references—an approach to Dante studies that has continued to the present day. Some of these earliest commentators, starting with Graziolo de' Bambaglioli in 1324, went further than that, taking the poem's claim to divine inspiration at face value (although the approach of Dante's son Pietro, writing some fifteen years later, was to consider the work as a fiction). This emphasis on the part of Graziolo and others did much to spread the poem's popularity and to endow it with an almost canonical status. Perhaps the most direct and succinct summation of this view is found in the words of Filippo Villani at the end of the fourteenth century: "I believe that no poet could have imagined such sublime and profound matters, or touched upon things which are so difficult for the human mind, or written so much poetry in the purest language, except by the inspiration of the Holy Spirit."

Another reason for the immediate acceptance and popularity of the *Comedy* can be found in its middle component, the *Purgatorio*. The concept of purgatory—the belief that there were some souls who had accepted grace and salvation before death but had still not sufficiently atoned for their sins—has always been a part of the Catholic (though not the Protestant) tradition, based on some biblical references to the value of praying for the souls of the dead. The church made its first official statement to this effect in 1274, but did not address the notion of purgatory as an actual place. *Tractatus de Purgatorio Sancti Patricii*, a work in Latin prose by an anonymous English monk, purporting to describe a trip to a physical purgatory undertaken by a repentant Irish knight, had been composed around 1180. But it took Dante's imaginative genius—and use of the common language—to fashion a vivid and realistic vision of purgatory as a mountain upon which souls are punished, on various levels organized according to the Seven Deadly Sins, in order to purge themselves of their imperfections and to do proper penance for their past transgressions.

Dante's overt purpose, especially in the *Inferno* and to some extent in the *Purgatorio*, is a kind of medieval "scared straight" program, accomplished in part through the promulgation of a rigid religious belief system. Of course, no one nowadays reads the *Inferno* in order to be instructed in the tenets of Catholicism, just as no one goes to *Moby-Dick* to learn the principles of seamanship. Besides, there is much in the poem's scale of values that may strike a contemporary sensibility as offensive—the severity of its strictures, its homophobia and anti-ecumenism, its emphasis on the necessity of Christian baptism and the consequent denial of salvation to unchristened infants and virtuous nonbelievers, including those who, like Virgil himself, had the misfortune to be born before Jesus Christ's lifetime. Clearly, any medieval work that had only these characteristics would be unloved, unremembered, and untranslated, its very existence known only to scholars and historians.

Even more clearly, this is not the case with Dante's poem. By 1380 the *Comedy* had been translated, perhaps a bit ironically, into Latin. At about the same time, in England, the writings of Geoffrey Chaucer contained a number of allusions to Dante. The most substantial of these was a retelling, in the Monk's Tale of the *Canterbury Tales*, of the tragic Ugolino episode from Cantos XXXII–XXXIII of the *Inferno*; at the conclusion of his rendering, Chaucer advises anyone who wishes for a longer account to read "the grete poete of Ytaille / That highte Dant, for he kan al devyse / Fro point to point, nat o word wol he faille." Translations of the

Comedy into both Catalan and Castilian appeared a little over a hundred years after Dante's death, and by the end of the fifteenth century it was translated into French. Yet, despite Chaucer's recommendation, for nearly half a millennium Britons who wanted to read the great poet of Italy had to learn his language in order to do so. The first extended translation into English of any passage of the *Inferno*—again the Ugolino episode, done in blank verse (unrhymed iambic pentameter) by Jonathan Richardson—appeared in 1719, and it was not until 1782 that a complete *Inferno*—also in blank verse, by Charles Rogers—was published in English. Whatever reasons may have been responsible for Dante's slow appearance in English, it has been more than made up for in the last two hundred years. The *Inferno* has been translated into English more frequently, by far, than into any other language, and the rate of that frequency seems to be increasing, with more than fifteen new translations having been published in the last quarter-century alone.

Before we consider several others of the excellent reasons for the widespread and enduring popularity of the *Inferno*, let us take a moment to appreciate just how extraordinary a phenomenon that popularity is. We are speaking, after all, about an intricately rhymed poem more than forty-seven hundred lines long. It abounds in biblical, classical, and mythological references, and contains some abstruse, and at times abstract, discussions of classical and early Christian philosophy. A good many of its characters and their situations cannot be fully understood without detailed reference to political and military events in thirteenth-century Florence. The *Iliad*, the *Odyssey*, and the *Aeneid* can all be enjoyed without going beyond the texts themselves, and translations of them are often published without annotations; an unannotated *Inferno*—even though there are several available—is almost unimaginable.

But, equally clearly, the *Inferno* has many other qualities that fully justify its standing as a masterpiece of world literature. To begin with, it is brilliantly executed. The style of the poem is an amazingly flexible and infinitely modulated instrument, ranging throughout the text from straightforward narrative to vivid description, from inspiring sublimity to shocking earthiness, from extravagant rhetorical figures to dialogue of intense and heartrending directness. There are the frequent and famous similes, ranging from a line or two to nearly a page, that appear throughout the text; the striking description of the Apulian battle dead at the beginning of Canto XXVIII, which leads into the hideous mutilations inflicted on the bodies of those sinners who created discord, is just one among many such examples. Comparisons drawn from topography, history, myth, and even domestic life serve, among other functions, to let some light and air into the claustrophobic chambers of hell and give the work an amplitude it might not otherwise possess. All of these, and more, Dante seeks to integrate into a comprehensive whole, so comprehensive that mythological figures are invested with a reality equal to that of historical ones.

Dante's Life

Dante Alighieri was born in Florence in 1265, sometime between mid-May and mid-June: he tells us in Canto XXII of the *Paradiso* that he was born under the sign of Gemini. Thus, in April 1300, when the *Inferno* is set, Dante was nearing his thirty-fifth birthday, which would place him exactly "midway through the journey" of the "threescore years and ten" that the Ninetieth Psalm describes as the span of a human life. While of modest financial circumstances, his family was of notable lineage; his great-great-grandfather Cacciaguida degli Elisei (whom he encounters among the blessed in the *Paradiso*) had been a cavalier and a crusader. While Dante was still young, both of his parents died—his mother, Gabriella, known as Bella, when he was still under ten years of age; his father, Alighiero di Bellincione degli Alighieri, a moneylender and a renter of property both in the city and beyond, when Dante was about eighteen. Dante's father remarried after Bella's death; sources differ as to how many children he had with each of his wives. In 1277, at the age of twelve, Dante was betrothed to Gemma di Manetto Donati. Their marriage, which took place around 1285, produced three sons, as well as a daughter who later became a nun under the name of Beatrice. Dante never mentions Gemma in his writings, and it has been traditionally, but not necessarily reliably, assumed that their relationship was not a close one.

According to Dante's own testimony in the *Vita nuova*, a gathering of thirty-one poems set within the framework of a narrative and a commentary upon them, the most important relationship of his life began when, at the age of nearly nine, he first beheld an eight-year-old girl named Beatrice. Beginning with one of the first biographies of Dante—written a quarter-century after his death by Giovanni Boccaccio, author of the *Decameron*—she has been identified with Beatrice Portinari, who married a wealthy banker named Simone de' Bardi, had several children, and died in 1290 at the age of twenty-four. But even if we had much more factual information, it would of course be impossible to determine the precise relation between autobiography and mythmaking in the *Vita nuova*—or, for that matter, in the *Comedy* itself. In the *Vita nuova*, which dates in all likelihood from his late twenties, Dante describes an intense love sustained on the slightest and most occasional of contacts, which gradually deepened and transformed itself as the lover came to terms with defects in his own nature, and which led to a resolve, after the death of the beloved, not to write of her again until he could do so in a way that would be worthy of her.

In his twenties and thirties, Dante took an increasingly active part in the public affairs of his city. In June 1289, he was a cavalryman at the battle of Campaldino, in which the Florentine forces routed those of the province of Arezzo. At that time, it was necessary to be enrolled in one of the city's professional guilds in order to take part in Florentine politics, so in 1295 Dante became a member of the Apothecaries' Guild, which was open to poets and men of learning. Over the next several years he spoke frequently in official meetings and was appointed to a number of municipal positions, including his selection in June 1300 as a prior, one of the city's six-member governing council. Dante had an active interest and involvement in politics throughout his adult life, which would culminate in the infliction of traumatic damage upon his public career and the entire course of his life through the machinations of his political enemies. It is not at all surprising, then, that he saw fit to place a number of those enemies, including some who were not even dead yet, at various levels of hell, or that a century's worth of political and military strife is thoroughly ingrained in the text and texture of the poem. Many of the dead souls encountered by Dante had taken part in the seemingly endless power struggles between two opposing factions: the Guelphs, who were supporters of the increasing temporal power of the papacy, and the Ghibellines, supporters of the empire as the legitimate secular authority. That controversy had begun in 1075, when Pope Gregory VII asserted that the papacy had authority over secular matters and leaders as well as spiritual ones. The Italian names of the opposing parties derived from the German factions of Welf and Waiblinger, whose struggle originated when the archbishops of Mainz and Cologne prevented the accession of Frederick of Swabia, the hereditary successor to the throne of the Holy Roman Empire, in 1125. Nearly a century later, the divisions which that struggle exposed began to inflame the city of Florence and there to take on a life of their own.

These tensions flared into open strife in 1215, when a Florentine nobleman was murdered to avenge the insult of his having broken his engagement to the daughter of another powerful family. For the next three quarters of a century, the two factions took turns expelling each other from the city and establishing control over its affairs. In 1266, the year after Dante's birth, Charles of Anjou, acting on behalf of the pope, opposed Manfred, illegitimate son of Emperor Frederick II, at the battle of Benevento. Frederick had been deposed by Pope Innocent IV in 1245 and died in 1250, leaving the imperial throne vacant until 1308. With Manfred's defeat and death, the Ghibellines were effectively destroyed as a political force in Florence, and the city thereafter enjoyed a quarter-century of relative stability. But in the 1290s, factionalism revived and the Guelphs were split into opposing groups: the Blacks, led by the wealthy and powerful Donati family, to whom Dante was related by marriage, and the Whites, who evolved into Ghibellines as Pope Boniface VIII sided with the Blacks in an effort to consolidate his power. Dante allied himself with the Whites, since he regarded the empire as the divine instrument of temporal authority and fiercely decried (including several times in the course of the *Inferno*) the corruption wrought within the church by its pursuit and exercise of secular power.

On June 9, 1301, Florence's city council took up a request by Pope Boniface VIII for two hundred cavalrymen to assist him in securing territories in southern Tuscany. While others expressed less than wholehearted enthusiasm, Dante was the only member of the council to speak out unequivocally against the proposal. In September, he angered the pope again when he refused to support Boniface's invitation of French forces into Italy. A month later, Dante was part of a three-man delegation sent to Rome to attempt to conciliate the pope. After their meeting, Dante was detained by Boniface and effectively prevented from returning home with his two companions. In his absence, on November 1, Charles of Valois, with the pope's backing, led his army into Florence and Dante's political enemies took complete control of the city. On January 27, 1302, Dante was tried and convicted in absentia on trumped-up charges of financial corruption and defiance of the pope, stripped of all his property, and banished from Florence. He refused to stoop to answering the charges against him, and, despite his sporadic hopes of negotiating an end to his exile, the banishment was later intensified to include a sentence of death should he be found inside the city. He never saw Florence again. (The city finally rescinded his death sentence in 2008.) As noted above, in the *Inferno* Dante took such revenge upon his enemies as he could. Boniface, who died in 1308, comes in for particular obloquy, with Dante missing no opportunity to abuse him for his corruption. Although Boniface was still alive in April 1300, when the poem takes place, in Canto XIX Dante shows us the precise spot in hell that is waiting for him.

In the years of his exile, Dante wandered restlessly through northern Italy, spending time in Lucca, Padua, and Bologna, taking up an extended residence (1312–18) in Verona, and settling finally in Ravenna, where he died, probably of malarial fever, on September 13, 1321. He began the *Inferno* around 1308, and completed it by 1314, when he had handwritten copies of the text made and circulated, the method of publication in the pre-Gutenberg era. Copies of the *Purgatorio* had begun to appear by 1318, and Dante finished writing the *Paradiso* only months before his death.

Dante in the *Inferno*

While the poem's themes are universal in scope—it is "the journey of our life," not just his own, that the poem's narrator is embarked upon—the detour on that journey that is recounted in the *Inferno* is uniquely Dante's own, and the fictional character who undertakes it shares his name and a great deal of his personal history with his creator. We have touched upon several instances of direct autobiographical details in the poem, but there are other times when the personal elements are indirect and subtle. In Canto XIII, for example, within the wood of the suicides Dante encounters Pier delle Vigne, who, by his own testimony, had been falsely accused of betraying his master, Emperor Frederick II. Imprisoned on these charges, Pier despaired of clearing his name and killed himself in his cell. Pier tells his story to Dante in the highly rhetorical style characteristic of his actual official documents and his poems, and then suddenly shifts to a direct, straightforward manner of expression as he utters a passionate plea to Dante to restore his good name upon Dante's return to earth. Surely this heartfelt passage is infused with Dante's own resentment and frustration at finding himself in similar circumstances. And then there is the extended episode of uproarious and occasionally scatological farce that takes up most of Cantos XXI and XXII, in which Dante and Virgil find themselves fallen among the crude and energetic demons called the *Malebranche*, or Evilclaws. In the uncharacteristic broad comedy of this interlude, we may very well see an attempt by Dante to use humor to distance himself from the pain of personal experience, since the kind of sin punished here—barratry, financial corruption, the selling of political offices and influence—is the very crime that he was treacherously convicted of.

One of the most striking aspects of the personal element in the *Inferno* is the way the protagonist is frequently torn between his feelings and his beliefs. Much of the time, he takes the thematically appropriate attitude of hostility to the damned, most notably in the cases of Vanni Fucci, the thief and blasphemer who remains as furious and offensive in death as he was in life (Cantos XXIV-XXV), and Bocca degli Abati (Canto XXXII), a Ghibelline sympathizer who betrayed the Guelphs at the battle of Montaperti in 1260. At other points, Dante's human sympathies overcome his Christian duty, as when he faints with emotion after hearing Francesca's sad account of her sinful relationship with her brother-in-law Paolo and their deaths at the hands of her husband, or when he movingly expresses his continuing devotion to his mentor Ser Brunetto Latini, who has been condemned for sodomy (Canto XV), or when he begins to weep at the sight of the deformed bodies of the soothsayers (Canto XX). For this last lapse, he is sternly rebuked by Virgil, for to pity those whom God has condemned is implicitly to wish their fate were different, and thus to dissent from God's judgments.

Yet there are a number of instances, such as the encounter with Francesca, in which Virgil allows Dante to indulge his sympathies, as well as several cases—the virtuous pagans in Canto IV, the heretic Farinata in Canto X, the sodomites in Canto XVI—in which Virgil goes so far as to instruct Dante to show deference and respect. The characterization of Virgil is an especially interesting facet of the poem. He is unmistakably portrayed as fully worthy of the reverence that Dante shows him, and yet there are several places at which he misunderstands a situation or shows poor judgment, and he is a study in barely suppressed fury when, at the end of Canto XXIII, he is openly mocked by one of the damned for having trusted the directions given him by the leader of the pack of demons.

Thus, it would appear that even in the afterlife it is impossible to avoid the infinite and often maddening complexities of the human spirit. Far from being a defect, this is one of the glories of Dante's poem. Like every great work of literature, the *Inferno* is above all a profoundly moving, profoundly human document. After we have read it, what we remember most vividly is its remarkable gallery of characters and the range of emotions that they display: Francesca, who even in hell seeks to portray herself as the helpless victim of irresistible urges; Farinata, who remains proudly convinced of the rightness of his actions and looks about him "as if hell itself were contemptible in his sight"; Ulysses, who acknowledges his inadequacies as son, husband, and father, but retains his unquenchable spirit of curiosity and quest; Master Adam, the forger (Canto XXX), who says, simply and poignantly, "Alive I had everything I wished, and here / one drop of water would be all to me"; Ugolino, whose anguished description of the deaths of his sons prompts him to cry out, "If not this, what could ever make you weep?"; and many more. Dante is the only character in the entire poem whose heart is still beating, and that heart goes on beating, loudly and clearly, to every reader of the *Inferno*.

A Note on the Text

It may be possible to produce a definitive translation of a novel, even a great novel, but poetry, with its rich and complex use of language and its tight interweaving of form and content, is a very different matter. One can easily imagine five or even ten translations of a single Rilke sonnet, all good in their own way, all reasonable approximations of at least some aspects of the original, and all substantially different from one another. With the *Inferno*, we are dealing not with a mere fourteen lines but with forty-seven hundred, in a book-length poem that not only tells a vivid, intricate story but also engages religion, morality, history, politics, myth, philosophy, psychology, and the author-protagonist's personal experiences. Matters of tone and diction, form and structure, are of critical importance. A work of such stunning artistry and complexity creates space enough not only for the translations already in the field, but for undreamt-of others as well.

The often striking differences among Dante translations can be explained by the different aspects of the original that they emphasize and the different audiences for which they are intended. Scholarly translations are principally concerned to render the paraphrasable content of the text as accurately and precisely as possible. Versions aimed at a general audience seek to capture the narrative and characterizations as directly, and often as simply, as they can. In both such instances, there is little if any concern with the poetic dimension, no attempt to reproduce the rhythmic and tonal effects of the original.

As a poet myself, I have sought to re-create the poetry of the *Inferno*, as I see it on the page and hear it my head when I read the original. To me, a large and necessary part of what this means is an attempt to re-create the *terza rima* structure. But it does not mean that I am less interested in the narrative or in any of the other aspects of the poem mentioned above, since, as I have said, the best poetry (and Dante's poetry fits that description as well as anyone's) is an interplay of form and content in which, ideally, neither element is made to suffer at the expense of the other. So far as I am aware, no other American translator of the past fifty years has attempted a fully rhymed version of the *Inferno*. Modern American translators of the poem, even those who are poets writing for an audience of poetry lovers, have, like most modern translators in general, chosen not to strictly reproduce the rhyme scheme of the original text. Some abandon rhyme (and some, even meter) altogether, while others try at least to suggest the nature of Dante's practice by a more sparing use of rhyme or with off-rhymes.

An ideal translation, which is of course impossible, would say everything that Dante says exactly as he says it, in exactly the same form that he employs. In attempting to approach that ideal as closely as possible, I have always translated poetry just as I have always written it, striving to achieve the blend of form and content that I spoke of earlier. To abandon or severely compromise the poem's form in the hope of honoring its content is, to my way of thinking, to destroy the balance necessary to achieve that blend. Thus, rather than begin with a hierarchy of values which dictates that some of the components of the original must be downplayed, or even eliminated, at the expense of others, I hope to salvage as high a percentage as I can of all the elements of the poem.

I reject the seeming premise of some mid-twentieth-century British translators that, as a medieval poet, Dante may be properly rendered into English through the constant use of archaic diction and inversion of word order, just as I reject the practice of certain translators who sought to enliven Dante's plainspokenness with rhetorical flourishes that are antithetical to his own practice and sensibility. I have tried to make poetry in the way that Dante does, which is, for the most part, through rhythm and sound. Rhythmically, I have employed a flexible pentameter that will in places be more reminiscent of Robert Frost or late Shakespeare than of Alexander Pope. This loosening of the strict metrical pattern, which still seeks to retain five strong beats in every line, seemed less out of place here than it might elsewhere, given the particular qualities of the *Inferno*—the frequent shifts of scene, mood, and tonal register; the intense interactions between Dante and the damned; the knockabout quality of some of the episodes.

In practical terms, my approach means that every problem of translation must be solved not by the unflinching imposition of some abstract theory or principle, but by the immediate needs, in context, of that particular moment of the poem. Sometimes that requires a literal approximation of Dante's statement; sometimes it demands the reproduction of a rhetorical figure or structure; and so on. Compromises are inevitable: the occasional resort to inexact rhymes; the compression or expansion of content to fit the pattern; the willingness to run over at either end of tercets that are self-contained in the original; and—again—so on. But I always kept in mind the harmony, integration, and clarity of the original in order to create as harmonious, integrated, and clear an approximation as I could. The beauty of the *Inferno* lies in its tiniest details and in its grand design, and in seeking to attend to both the details and the design, I hope that I have managed to convey something of that beauty to the readers of this translation.

To those seriously interested in the subject of English translation of Dante, I would recommend the following works: Gilbert F. Cunningham, The Divine Comedy *in English: A Critical Bibliography* (two volumes, 1965 and 1966): a thorough, detailed, shrewd, and at times hilarious evaluation of every English translation of at least one of the three parts of the *Comedy*; Eric Griffiths and Matthew Reynolds, eds., *Dante in English* (2005): an anthology of excerpts, from Chaucer to now, from great poets to obscure scribblers, illustrating how Dante has been translated, adapted, imitated, and used as an inspiration for original poems; and Tim Smith and Marco Sonzogni, eds., *To Hell and Back: An Anthology of Dante's* Inferno *in English Translation (1782–2017)* (2017): a compilation of two complete versions of the *Inferno* and two bonus cantos, made up of one entire canto from each of seventy different translators, showcasing the full range of approaches taken and providing a number of interesting and otherwise inaccessible texts.

Map: Dante's Hell

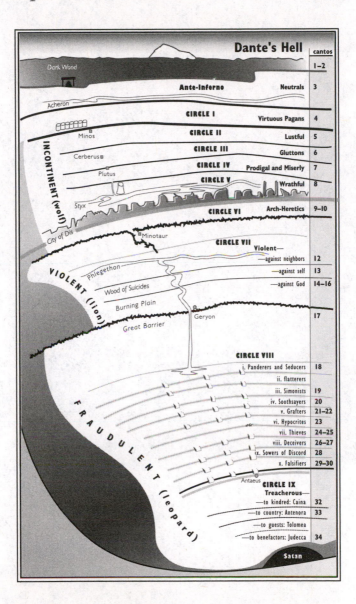

Dante

Inferno

Canto I

The Dark Wood; The Three Beasts; Virgil's Appearance;
The Prophecy of the Greyhound

Midway through the journey of our life,° I found
    myself in a dark wood, for I had strayed
    from the straight pathway to this tangled ground.   3
How hard it is to tell of, overlaid
    with harsh and savage growth, so wild and raw
    the thought of it still makes me feel afraid.   6
Death scarce could be more bitter. But to draw
    the lessons of the good that came my way,
    I will describe the other things I saw.   9
Just how I entered there I cannot say,
    so full of sleep when I began to veer
    that I did not see that I had gone astray   12
from the one true path. But once I had drawn near
    the bottom of a hill at the far remove
    of the valley that had pierced my heart with fear,   15
I saw its shoulders mantled from above
    by the warm rays of the planet that gives light
    to guide our steps, wherever we may rove.°   18
At last I felt some calming of the fright
    that had allowed the lake of my heart no rest

while I endured the long and piteous night.   21
And as a drowning man with heaving chest
   escapes the current and, once safe on shore,
   turns back to see the dangers he has passed,   24
so too my mind, still lost in flight, once more
   turned back to see the passage that had never
   let anyone escape alive before.   27
I paused to let my weary limbs recover,
   and then began to climb the lone hillside,
   my fixed foot always lower than the other.°   30
But I had hardly started when I spied
   a leopard in my pathway, lithe and fleet,
   all covered with a sleek and spotted hide.   33
And as I faced it, it would not retreat,
   but paced before me and so blocked my way
   that more than once I had to turn my feet   36
to retrace my steps. It was the break of day,°
   the sun was mounting in the morning sky
   with the same stars as when that whole array   39
of lovely things was first given movement by
   divine love. The sweet season of the year
   and the hour made me think that I might try   42
to evade that bright-skinned beast as it came near,
   but then I felt my good hopes quickly fade
   and in an instant I was numbed with fear   45
to see a lion in my path that made
   straight for me, head held high and ravenous,
   and seemed to make the very air afraid.   48
And a she-wolf too, that in its leanness was
   laden with every craving. Those who seek
   fulfillment there find only wretchedness.   51
The sight of this one made me feel so weak,
   so overcome with dread, that instantly
   I lost all hope of climbing to the peak.   54
As a man is eager in prosperity
   but when time brings him losses can be found

giving way to weeping and to misery, 57
so did I feel as the she-wolf pressed me round
　　so relentlessly that bit by bit I stepped
　　back where the sun is mute on the low ground.° 60
And as I drove myself into the depth,
　　a shape was offered to my vision, wan
　　as if from a long silence it had kept. 63
Seeing him in that great desert, I began
　　to call out. "*Miserere*—on me," I cried,
　　"whatever you are, a shade or a solid man!" 66
"Not man, although I was a man," he replied.
　　"My parents were both Mantuans. I descend
　　from those of Lombardy on either side. 69
I was born *sub Julio,* at the latter end.°
　　Under the good Augustus I lived in Rome
　　in the days when false and lying gods still reigned. 72
I was a poet, and I sang of him,
　　Anchises' righteous son, who sailed from Troy
　　after the burning of proud Ilium.° 75
But why do you turn back toward trouble? Why
　　do you not ascend the delectable mount instead,
　　the origin and cause of every joy?" 78
"Are you that Virgil then, that fountainhead
　　that spills such a mighty stream of eloquence?"
　　I said this with a shame-filled brow, and said: 81
"Light and glory of all poets, may my intense
　　love and long study of your poetry
　　avail me now for my deliverance. 84
You are my master, my authority,
　　for it is from you alone that I learned to write
　　in the noble style that has so honored me. 87
You see why I have turned back from the height.
　　Illustrious sage, please help me to confound
　　this beast that makes my pulses shake with fright." 90
"It were best to go another way around,"
　　he answered, seeing tears start from my eyes,

"if your hope is to escape this savage ground,   93
because this creature that provokes your cries
    allows no man to get the best of her,
    but blocks each one, attacking till he dies.   96
Of such a vile and vicious character
    and greedy appetite, she is never sated,
    and when she has fed is even hungrier.   99
Many the animals with whom she has mated.
    Her couplings—till her painful deathblow is dealt
    by the greyhound—will continue unabated.   102
This greyhound will not feed on land or wealth,
    but on virtue, love, and wisdom. He will be
    born in the region between felt and felt.°   105
He will restore low-lying Italy,
    for which Euryalus, Turnus, the maid Camilla,
    and Nisus gave their life's blood.° Tirelessly   108
he will track the beast through every town until
    he comes at last to drive her back into
    that hell from which she sprang at Envy's will.   111
Therefore I think it would be best for you
    to follow me. I will be your guide, and I
    will lead you out of here and take you through   114
an eternal place where you will be greeted by
    the shriekings of despair and you will see
    ancient tormented spirits as they cry   117
aloud at the second death. Then you will be
    with those who are content within the fire,
    for they hope to join the blest eventually.   120
You will see those blest, if that is your desire,
    with a worthier soul than I.° Into her hands
    I will entrust you when I can go no higher.   123
That emperor who presides above commands,
    since I did not heed his law, that none may gain
    entrance through me to where his city stands.°   126
His rule is everywhere. There is his reign,
    his city, and his throne! Happy are they

whom he chooses to inhabit that domain!"   129
"Poet," I said to him, "so that I may
    escape this harm and worse that may await,
    in the name of that God you never knew, I pray   132
you lead me out to see Saint Peter's gate°
    and all those souls that you have told me of,
    who must endure their miserable state."   135
I followed him as he began to move.

Canto II

*The Evening of Good Friday, April the 8th; The Doubts of the
Pilgrim; The Journeys of Saint Paul and Aeneas; Beatrice
Summons Virgil; The Beginning of the Pilgrim's Descent*

The day was waning, and the darkening sky
    called all the creatures of the earth to rest
    after the long day's labors. Only I   3
was preparing all alone to endure the test
    of the journey and the pity of what I would see,
    as unerring memory will now attest.   6
Muses, high genius, aid me! Memory,
    that recorded what I saw among the dead,
    here you will show your true integrity.°   9
"O poet, you who are my guide," I said,
    "weigh whether I am fit for what lies in wait
    before you entrust me to the path ahead.   12
Of Silvius's father° you narrate
    how he saw the immortal world with his mortal sense
    while still immured in our corrupted state.   15
That evil's foe showed him such preference,
    aware of the result that it would bring,
    of who and what would come as consequence—   18
to a thoughtful mind this seems a proper thing.

Empyrean heaven in her high decrees
    chose him to be the father of fostering   21
Rome and her empire. Truly, both of these
    were founded to be the holy ground whereon
    the successor to great Peter keeps the keys.   24
On his journey which you celebrate, he was shown
    and told of things that served as the foundation
    of his victory and of the papal throne.   27
The Chosen Vessel then brought confirmation,
    by journeying there, of the true faith that must be
    the beginning of the path to our salvation.°   30
But why must I? On whose authority?
    I am not Aeneas, not Paul. Why should I seek
    what neither I nor anyone thinks me   33
worthy to do? Why start upon a bleak
    and, I fear, foolish journey? You are filled
    with wisdom, and hear more clearly than I speak."   36
Like someone who unwills what he has willed,
    and with new thoughts sees his resolve go by,
    letting what was begun go unfulfilled,   39
so, standing on that shadowy slope, was I.
    Rethinking what with such impulsiveness
    I had begun, I let my impulse die.   42
"If I have rightly comprehended this,"
    the shade of that magnanimous soul replied,
    "your spirit has been seized by cowardice,   45
which has often harried men and nullified
    many a worthy enterprise, as when
    a beast will see a shadow and turn aside.   48
To free you from this fear, let me explain
    why I have come, and tell you of the request
    that first made me take pity on your pain.   51
I was among the suspended ones when a blest
    and lovely lady called me. So fair was she,
    I begged that I might serve at her behest.   54
Brighter than stars, her eyes shone brilliantly,

and in a tone so sweet and soft and pure,
   with an angel's voice, I heard her say to me: 57
'O gentle Mantuan soul, with fame secure
   in the world above, whose name will still resound
   as long as the world continues to endure,   60
my friend, who is not fortune's friend, has found
   so many obstacles upon his way
   up the desert slope that fear has turned him round.   63
I fear, from all that I have heard them say
   in heaven, that I have made too late a start,
   that already he has gone too far astray.   66
Go now and, with the words of your high art
   and the skill to rescue him from this distress,
   assist him and bring solace to my heart.   69
I who now send you forth am Beatrice.
   I have come from a place I long to see again.
   Love prompted me. Love makes me ask you this.   72
How often I will speak to praise you when
   I stand before my Lord upon his throne.'
   She said no more, and I responded then: 75
'O lady of virtue, through whose power alone
   humanity is able to rise higher
   than all within the least-circling heaven's zone,°   78
I am so pleased to do what you desire
   that were it already done, it would be late.
   All you need do is say what you require.   81
But how is it that you did not hesitate
   to leave that longed-for spacious place on high
   and descend into this center where we wait?'   84
'Since you have such deep desire to know why
   I am not at all afraid to venture here,'
   she told me, 'I will briefly clarify.   87
The only things that should inspire fear
   are those that can inflict an injury.
   The rest need not oppress us, it is clear.   90
God's grace has made me so I cannot be

moved in my heart by all your suffering
 or touched by all the flames surrounding me. 93
In heaven a noble lady,° pitying
 that great distress I send you to repair,
 has made a breech in the strict reckoning 96
that rules above. She summoned Lucia° there,
 and said:—Your follower, who is faithful still,
 needs you, and I commend him to your care.— 99
Lucia, who is the enemy of all
 cruelty, came immediately to the place
 where I was sitting with the venerable 102
Rachel,° and said:—Beatrice, God's true praise,
 why do you not help him who loved you so
 that he forsook the crowd and its crass ways? 105
Do you not hear him crying out below?
 Do you not see Death battle him by that flood
 the mighty ocean cannot overthrow?— 108
Never on earth did any seize his good
 or flee his harm as quickly as I flew,
 once I had heard such words and understood, 111
leaving my heavenly seat to come to you,
 trusting your words of such nobility
 that they honor you and all who hear them too.' 114
She turned when she had spoken. I could see
 tears shining in her eyes, making me still
 more eager to fulfill her charge to me. 117
So I have come to you, as was her will,
 saving you from the beast that blocked your way
 along the short path up the lovely hill. 120
What is this, then? Why, why do you delay,
 why does your heart make room for cowardice,
 why not be bold and resolute, when they, 123
those three great ladies of high blessedness
 in heaven's court, are keeping you in sight,
 when I promise you great good to come of this?" 126
As flowers droop and close in the chill of night,

then stand and open out upon the stem
    when the sun returns and touches them with light,   129
so my exhausted strength revived like them
    and, feeling courage rush into my heart,
    like one who has been set free I said to him: 132
"How compassionate she was, who took my part!
    How courteous you were, who quickly went
    in response to her true plea. Now let us start,   135
for the forcefulness of what you say has sent
    my heart new eagerness to go with you,
    reawakening my original intent.   138
Lead on. There is one will between us two.
    You are my guide, my lord and master." Thus
    I spoke. And when he moved, I entered too   141
the pathway through the savage wilderness.

Canto III

The Gate of Hell; The Neutral Angels; Charon; Dante Faints

THROUGH ME THE WAY TO THE CITY OF DESOLATION,
    THROUGH ME THE WAY TO EVERLASTING PAIN,
    THROUGH ME THE WAY TO SOULS IN ABOMINATION.   3
    JUSTICE MOVED MY GREAT MAKER IN MY DESIGN.
        I WAS CREATED BY THE PRIMAL LOVE,
        WISDOM SUPREME AND POTENCY DIVINE.   6
        BEFORE ME NOTHING WAS CREATED SAVE
        THE ETERNAL, AND I ENDURE ETERNALLY.
        ALL YOU WHO ENTER, LET NO HOPE SURVIVE.   9
In darkly colored letters I could see
    these words inscribed on a portal overhead.
    "Master," I said, "this saying is hard for me."   12
Like one who knows and understands, he said:
    "Here all your doubt is to be left behind,
    here all your cowardice is to fall dead.   15
Now we are in the place where you will find
    the ones I told you of, the wretched race
    of those who have lost the good use of the mind."   18
And then, with his hand on mine, and on his face
    a cheerful look that helped to calm my fears,
    he led me down into that secret place.   21

Sighs and laments and loud wails filled my ears.
  Those cries resounding through the starless air
  so moved me at first that I burst into tears.   24
A babble of tongues, harsh outcries of despair,
  noises of rage and grief, the beating of hands,
  and shrill and raucous voices everywhere   27
all made a mad uproar that never ends,
  revolving in that timeless darkened breeze
  the way a whirlwind whips the desert sands.   30
"Master, what do I hear? And who are these,"
  I cried, as the horror swirled around my head,°
  "who seem so shattered by their agonies?"   33
"This is the miserable estate," he said,
  "of the sorry souls of those who lived and died
  winning neither praise nor blame for the lives they'd led.°   36
They are mixed with the base angels who stood aside,
  who neither hastened to their Lord's defense
  nor rose against him in rebellious pride.   39
Heaven repels them lest its magnificence
  be tarnished, and they are turned away by hell
  lest sinners exalt themselves at their expense."   42
"Master," I said, "why do they thrash and yell?
  What is the fate that makes them carry on?"
  He answered: "I will very briefly tell.   45
They have no hope of death's oblivion.
  Because theirs is a life so blind and low,
  they are envious of every other one.   48
Mercy and justice scorn them. The world lets no
  report of them remain, not even a trace.
  Let us not speak of them, but look and go."   51
Looking again, I saw a banner race,
  whirling about so madly that it seemed
  unfit to make a stand in one fixed place.   54
Following it a line of people streamed,
  an endless line as far as I could see.
  That death had undone so many, I had not dreamed.   57

There were some among them who were known to me,
    and I saw the shade of him whose cowardice
    made him make the great refusal.° Instantly   60
I understood beyond a doubt that this
    was that craven company whom all despise,
    that God and his enemies find odious.   63
Those souls who had never lived, whose lives were lies,
    were naked, and were harried through their paces
    by swarms of stinging wasps and biting flies.   66
Blood mingling with their tears ran down their faces
    and splashed the earth around them, where it fed
    disgusting worms that wriggled in their traces.   69
Then I saw a crowd of people up ahead
    on the bank of a broad river. "What do I see,
    Master, who are those people there," I said,   72
"what compulsion makes them wait so eagerly
    for the chance to cross the river and be gone—
    or so in this dim light it seems to me."   75
And he replied: "These things will be made known
    when we must still our steps a while before
    we go across the somber Acheron."   78
Afraid I might offend, I said no more,
    but walked with eyes downcast, and shame-filled too,
    until we found ourselves upon the shore.   81
An old man white with age in a boat that drew
    toward where we all were gathered gave a cry:
    "Woe unto you, you miserable crew   84
of sinners! Put all hope of heaven by!
    I take you to the other shore, to the land
    of heat and cold, where darkness cannot die.   87
And you there, you who are still living, stand
    aside from all those others who are dead."
    But when I did not follow his command,   90
"By another way, by other ports," he said,
    "not here, you will be brought across to shore.
    A lighter craft will carry you instead."   93

My leader told him, "Charon,° no need to roar.
    Thus it is willed where there is power to do
    what has been willed, so question it no more."   96
This stopped the grizzled chops of the boatman who
    ferried the dead across the marshy river.
    Around his eyes two flaming circles flew.   99
But those weary, naked souls began to shiver,
    teeth gnashing, color gone from every face,
    at the harsh tirade that they'd heard him deliver.   102
They blasphemed God, they cursed the human race,
    their parents, the father's seed, the mother's womb,
    their birth, and even its very time and place.   105
Then they all drew together in the gloom,
    and weeping loudly they began to go
    to the evil shore that waits for all to whom   108
the fear of God means nothing. Eyes aglow
    like live coals, demon Charon herds them now
    and with his oar beats those who are too slow.   111
As one by one the leaves drop from the bough
    when autumn comes, and branches watch them fall
    till the earth has all their treasures, that is how   114
it was with Adam's evil seed. They all,
    one at a time, when signaled, left the shore,
    just as a bird will answer to its call.   117
So they cross the murky water, and before
    they have even landed on the other side,
    a new crowd gathers on this bank once more.   120
"My son," said my courteous master, "those who have died
    in the wrath of God all come together here
    from every country, eager now to ride   123
across the river as their time draws near.
    As God's own justice works upon them, they
    begin to feel desire in place of fear.   126
No worthy spirit ever comes this way,
    so if Charon complained about you, it should be
    clear to you now just what his words convey."   129

And then the dark plain shook so violently
    that I start to bathe in sweat all over again
    reliving the terror in my memory.   132
Up from the tear-soaked ground a great wind ran,
    flashing a bright red light out of its swell
    that blasted all my senses, and like a man   135
that sleep has overtaken, down I fell.

Canto IV

The First Circle; The Virtuous Heathen; Christ's Harrowing of
Hell; Meeting with the Poets of Classical Antiquity; Limbo

A crashing thunderclap made me awaken,
    putting the thick sleep in my head to rout.
    I started up like someone roughly shaken   3
out of a slumber. Standing, I looked about,
    gazing and turning my rested eyes around
    in every direction, trying to make out   6
just where I was. The truth is, I soon found
    I was standing on the edge of the abyss
    of pain, where roars of endless woe resound.   9
It was so dark and deep, so nebulous,
    I could see nothing in the depths although
    I stared intently from the precipice.   12
"Now let us descend into the blind world below,"
    the poet said, appearing pale and drawn.
    "I will be first, you second, as we go."   15
Seeing his pallor, I said: "I lean upon
    your strength when I falter, when I am afraid.
    If you are frightened, how shall I go on?"   18
"The anguish of the people here," he said,
    "colors my face in ways you read amiss,

thinking the pity that I feel is dread.   21
But let us go. The long road beckons us."
    And so he went, and had me follow, where
    the first circle runs, surrounding the abyss.   24
I heard no wails of lamentation there,
    no loud complaints, only the sound of sighs
    that agitated the eternal air.   27
From a sadness without torments rose the cries
    of children and of women and of men.
    Many and vast were the crowds before my eyes.   30
"Do you not ask," said my good master then,
    "what spirits these may be that fill this place?
    I will have you know, before we walk again,   33
they did not sin. But their merit won no grace
    because they lacked baptism, which must be
    the gateway to the faith that you embrace.   36
Those who preceded Christianity
    did not worship God according to his law,
    and I myself am of this company.   39
For this defect, and for no other flaw,
    we are lost, with this one punishment laid on,
    that without hope we feel desire gnaw."   42
Great sadness gripped my heart when he had done.
    Among those suspended in that limbo were
    many a worthy, honorable one.   45
"Tell me, my master," I said then, "tell me, sir,"
    feeling a need to be assured anew
    of the faith that conquers all ideas that err,   48
"did any ever leave here for heaven, through
    their own or another's merit?" And he said,
    seeing what my covert words were leading to: 51
"When I was newly placed among these dead,
    a mighty one came among us, whom I saw
    wearing the sign of victory on his head.   54
He took the shade of our first progenitor,
    Abel his son, and Noah, and God-honoring

Moses who was the giver of the law,   57
patriarch Abraham and David the king,
   Israel with his father and his sons
   and Rachel, for whom he did much laboring.°   60
He blessed all these and other paragons.
   And I would have you know that till that day
   no souls were saved. They were the earliest ones."°   63
We did not stop, but went along our way
   while he was speaking, passing now through some
   thick woods—not woods made out of trees, I say,   66
but of crowding spirits. We were not far from
   the place where I had slept so deeply, when
   I saw a dark hemisphere that was overcome   69
by a fiery light. Though still a bit distant then,
   we were close enough that I could see in part
   that the ground was held by honorable men.   72
I said: "O you who honor science and art,
   who are those men who even in this place
   possess such honor that sets them apart?"   75
And he: "Their fame, which time does not erase,
   still resounding in your world this very day,
   allows them to advance through heaven's grace."   78
Meanwhile I heard a voice before me say:
   "Hail to the highest poet! His honorable
   shade has returned to us, which had gone away."   81
Then when the voice had finished and was still,
   I saw four noble shades all moving forward,
   their faces neither glad nor sorrowful.   84
Said my master: "See the one who bears the sword,
   the one who walks before the other three
   acknowledged as their leader and their lord.   87
Homer the sovereign of all bards is he.°
   Horace the satirist is the second one.°
   Ovid comes third, and Lucan finally.°   90
Because, along with me, they all have won
   the name by which I was just now addressed,

they do me honor, and it is well done."   93
Assembled there before me were the best
    of poets, the school of that sweet lord of style
    who like an eagle soars above the rest.   96
When they had talked together for a while,
    they turned to me with a nod of salutation,
    at which I saw my master broadly smile.   99
And then they made far greater demonstration
    of honor, bringing me up to their height,
    making me sixth in their wisdom's congregation.°   102
So we walked onward, moving toward the light,
    and the things that were said among us it is good
    not to say here, as to say them there was right.   105
We came to where a noble castle stood
    circled by seven high walls. All around
    that citadel a lovely streamlet flowed.   108
We crossed the stream as though on solid ground.
    Through seven gates those sages passed with me.
    We came to a fresh green meadow, where we found   111
people with looks of great authority,
    whose eyes moved slowly and were serious,
    who spoke in quiet tones, infrequently.   114
Then we moved off to one side, where there was
    a luminous broad hillside that would yield
    a view of the whole gathering to us.   117
Before me on that green enameled field
    such glorious spirits appeared that I still prize
    within my soul the sights that were revealed.   120
I saw Electra, and could recognize
    Aeneas and Hector° among those with her,
    and armored Caesar with his hawklike eyes.   123
I saw Camilla and Penthesilea° there,
    and I saw King Latinus sitting in
    another place, with his daughter Lavinia° near.   126
I saw that Brutus who overthrew Tarquin.
    Lucretia, Cornelia, Julia, and with these three

was Marcia. Alone, apart, was Saladin.°   129
And lifting my eyes higher, I could see,
    seated, the master of all those who know,
    amid his philosophic family.   132
All of them gaze upon him, all of them show
    all honor to him. Plato and Socrates
    stand closest to him. I saw row on row,   135
Anaxagoras, Thales, and Diogenes,
    Heraclitus, Zeno, and Democritus
    who imputes the world to chance, Empedocles,   138
Dioscorides° who collected things' essences,
    Hippocrates, Galen,° the moral philosopher
    Seneca, Cicero, Linus, and Orpheus,°   141
Ptolemy, Euclid the geometer,°
    Avicenna, and Averroës° whose monument
    is the great commentary. So many of them there were,   144
I cannot describe them to the full extent,
    for often, with my long theme to set the pace,
    the telling must fall short of the event.   147
We six become two. Out of the quiet space,
    through another route into the trembling air,
    now my wise guide has led me to a place   150
where there is nothing shining anywhere.

Canto V

Thus I went down from where the first circle lies
    into the second, which surrounds less space
    but much more pain, provoking wails and cries.   3
There Minos° stands with his horrid snarling face.
    He examines the sinners at the entranceway.
    Entwining, he assigns each one its place.   6
Each misbegotten soul, that is to say,
    confesses all as it faces him, and so
    that connoisseur of sinfulness can weigh   9
how far each spirit will be sent below.
    Each time his tail coils round him indicates
    another level that the soul must go.   12
Always a swarming multitude awaits.
    They tell, they hear, they are hurled into the air,
    flung one by one to their eternal fates.   15
Minos addressed me when he saw me there,
    halting the meting out of punishments:
    "O you who come to this house of pain, beware   18
how you enter and where you place your confidence.
    Do not let yourself be fooled by the wide door!"

And my leader: "Why do you too take offense?   21
Do not obstruct the path he is fated for.
    Thus it is willed where there is power to do
    what has been willed, so question it no more."   24
Now all the mournful sounds are starting to
    surround and overwhelm me. Now I arrive
    where the roar of lamentation runs me through.   27
Here the light is mute and the atmosphere alive
    with the noise of constant howling, like the sea
    under assault by violent gusts that strive   30
with one another. The hellish wind blows free,
    sweeping the spirits headlong through the air.
    It whirls and pounds and mauls them endlessly.   33
It carries them back before the ruin,° where
    they shriek and moan and utter their laments
    and curse the almighty power that sent them there.   36
The souls condemned to bear these punishments,
    I learned, are the carnal sinners, of lust so strong
    that they let it master reason and good sense.   39
As large, dense flocks of starlings are borne along
    by their wings in the cold season of the year,
    just so that blast propels the sinful throng,   42
drives them now up, now down, now there, now here.
    No hope consoles them, whether for repose
    or even for their pain to be less severe.   45
As it may happen that we see long rows
    of cranes above us as they chant their lay,
    so I saw spirits crying out their woes   48
as the wild windstorm carried them our way,
    till I said: "Master, all these souls I see
    lashed onward by the black air, who are they?"   51
"The first of those," my master said to me,
    "of whom you wish to hear was an empress
    over many languages in antiquity.   54
She was so enslaved by lust, so lecherous,
    that to keep the blame for her misdeeds at bay

her laws gave license to licentiousness.   57
She is Semíramis, who, as histories say,
  succeeded her husband Ninus as ruler of
  all of the lands where the sultan reigns today.°   60
Next is the one who killed herself for love
  and betrayed Sichaeus's ashes.° Here the bold
  Cleopatra comes, whom wanton passions drove.°   63
See Helen, for whom such dreadful years unrolled.
  See the great Achilles. In the end he came
  to battle love.° Behold Paris, and behold   66
Tristan°—" More than a thousand, and all the same—
  love took them from our life. And one and all
  he showed to me and told me each one's name.   69
And as I listened to my teacher call
  the list of each high lady and grand knight,
  I was overwhelmed, and I felt my senses fall   72
to pity. "Poet," I told him, "if I might,
  I willingly would speak now to those two
  who are paired. Upon the wind they seem so light."   75
"The wind will bring them into closer view,"
  he said, "and you must call them, when it does,
  by the love that leads them. They will come to you."   78
When the wind had turned them near to where I was,
  "O weary spirits," I began to cry,
  "if another does not forbid, come speak with us!"   81
As doves with wings held steady and raised high
  are called by desire back to the sweet nest
  and carried by their will across the sky,   84
so from the flock of Dido and the rest
  they came through the evil air to where we stood,
  through the power of my compassionate request.   87
"O living creature, gracious and so good
  that through this black air you have dared to go
  to visit us who stained the world with blood,   90
if the king of the universe were not our foe,
  then we would surely pray to him to fill

your heart with peace for pitying our woe.   93
We will speak and hear of whatever it is your will
    to speak and hear of, while the wind will permit,
    as it is doing now, by keeping still.   96
The place where I was born° is the city set
    along the shore where the Po descends to be
    at peace at last with those that follow it.   99
Love, which in gentle hearts flares rapidly,
    seized this one for my lovely body—how
    it was violently stripped away still injures me.   102
Love, which, when one is loved, does not allow
    that it be refused, seized me with joy in him,
    which, as you see, is with me even now.   105
Love led us to a single death. The grim
    Caïna waits to claim our murderer."°
    These words were borne across to us from them.   108
When I had heard those afflicted souls, there were
    long minutes while I stood and bowed my head,
    until the poet's question made me stir: 111
"What are you thinking?" When I spoke, I said:
    "How strong desires and thoughts of sweet allure
    have brought them to this grievous pass instead!"   114
And then I turned to face those souls once more:
    "Stinging tears of pain and pity fill my eyes,
    Francesca, for the torments you endure.   117
But tell me how you came to recognize
    those dubious desires. How did love show
    its purpose in the hour of sweet sighs?"   120
And she replied: "There is no greater woe
    than looking back on happiness in days
    of misery. Your guide can tell you so.   123
But if you are so eager to retrace
    our love's first root, then I will make it known
    as one who speaks with tears upon her face.   126
In reading how Lancelot had been overthrown
    by love,° we chanced to pass the time one day.

We sat, suspecting nothing, all alone.   129
Some of the things we read made our eyes stray
    to one another's and the color flee
    our faces, but one point swept us away.   132
We read how that smile desired so ardently
    was kissed by such a lover, one so fine,
    and this one, who will never part from me,   135
trembling all over pressed his mouth on mine.
    The book was a Gallehault,° the author as well.
    That day we did not read another line."   138
And while she told the tale she had to tell,
    the other wept. I fainted where I stood
    out of pity, as if dying, and I fell   141
down on the ground the way a dead man would.

Canto VI

The Third Circle: The Gluttonous; Cerberus;
Ciacco; Civil War in Florence

With my sense restored, which had deserted me
    at the pitiful condition of that pair
    of kinsfolk, stunned by their sad history,   3
I start to see new torments everywhere
    and new tormented souls, wherever I range
    or turn myself, wherever I may stare.   6
I have come to the third circle, where the strange
    damned freezing rainfall endlessly pours down,
    whose quality and measure never change.   9
A mass of hail and snow and filthy brown
    water comes streaming through the murky air,
    and as it lands it putrefies the ground.   12
The weird and savage Cerberus° is there,
    his three throats barking doglike at the dead
    who lie submerged and sodden everywhere.   15
With a black and greasy beard, eyes burning red,
    gross belly and huge clawlike hands, he flogs
    and flays and quarters and rips them all to shreds.   18
The constant rainfall makes them howl like dogs.
    One side provides the other one's defense

as the wretches twist and turn inside their bogs.   21
The great worm Cerberus saw us and at once
    bared the fangs of his three mouths, and never ceased
    moving his limbs, all quivering and tense.   24
My master stretched his open hands and seized
    great clumps of earth, and quickly flung the foul
    gobbets right down the throats of the greedy beast.   27
Just as a hungry hound begins to howl
    and then grows quiet when his food is thrown
    to him, and strains at it with a low growl,   30
so too the demon Cerberus's own
    smeared faces hushed, that otherwise would roar
    to make the dead wish they were deaf as stone.   33
Where shades were flattened by the hard downpour,
    we set our steps upon the emptiness
    that still looked like the men they'd been before.   36
All of the shapes were lying in the mess,
    except for one that lifted up its head
    and sat itself upright to watch us pass.   39
"O you who are being led through hell," he said,
    "come close to me and name me if you can,
    for you were made before I was unmade."   42
"It may be that your suffering," I began,
    "has driven you from my memory, because
    you seem to me to be an unknown man.   45
But tell me who you are, set in such loss
    and desolation that, although there might
    be greater torments, none could be more gross."   48
He said: "Your native city, stuffed so tight
    with envy that the sack has overflowed,
    contained me too, back in the days of light.   51
Ciacco's the name you citizens bestowed
    on me.° For my damned sin of gluttony
    I'm pounded by the rainfall's filthy load.   54
Nor am I the only one. These that you see
    pay the same price for the same sin, one and all

forever." And he said no more to me.   57
"Ciacco," I said, "your miseries appall,
    stirring my heart till I could weep for pity.
    But tell me, if you know, what will befall   60
the citizens of our divided city,
    and if there be one just man, and why the knife
    of discord has so rent its soul already."   63
He answered: "Blood will follow after strife,
    the rustic sect will drive the other one
    out of the city, with much loss of life.   66
Before the third full circle of the sun
    the vanquished will turn vanquishers. Through dint
    of one upon the fence, this will be done.   69
Their standard will be long in the ascent.
    They'll oppress the others, who will not be freed
    however much they bristle and lament.   72
Two men are just, but no one pays them heed.
    Those people's hearts are set aflame by three
    sparks only—envy, arrogance, and greed."°   75
Thus far he spoke his doleful prophecy.
    I told him: "I would hear more. Once again
    with the great gift of your words enlighten me.   78
Of Tegghiaio and Farinata, worthy men,
    Arrigo, Mosca, Rusticucci, as well
    as many another benevolent citizen,   81
I want to hear whatever you can tell,
    for I truly wish to discover if they share
    the honey of heaven or taste the venom of hell."   84
"Their separate sins," he said, "have dragged them where
    some of the very blackest spirits stay.
    Keep going down and you will see them there.°   87
But when you see the sweet world again, I pray
    that you bring me to men's memory once more.
    Nothing else will I answer, nothing will I say."   90
His eyes, that had looked so steadily, now wore
    a squint. He stared at me, then bent his head

and lay down with the other blind ones as before.   93
"He will not stir again," my leader said,
   "until the angelic trump, when he will see
   that angry power that all the wicked dread.   96
Each will return to his sad tomb to be
   united with his substance and his form
   and hear the sounding of eternity."   99
Thus we moved slowly through the sodden scum,
   the filthy mix of spirits and of rain,
   talking a little of the life to come.   102
I asked him: "Master, will this burning pain
   be even greater come the judgment day,
   or stay just as it is, or will it wane?"   105
And he replied: "What does your science say?°
   The more a thing approaches to perfection,
   more pleasure or more pain will come its way.   108
Because these people suffer God's rejection,
   they never can be perfect, but are meant
   in future to be moved in that direction."   111
Along the circle of the path we went,
   speaking of more than I repeat, till we
   arrived at where it started its descent.   114
There we met Plutus, the great enemy.°

Canto VII

*The Fourth Circle: Misers and Spendthrifts;
The Wheel of Fortune; The Fifth Circle:
The Wrathful and Slothful*

"Pape Satàn, pape Satàn aleppe!"°
    Plutus began to cry with a harsh cluck.
    That gentle and all-knowing sage then kept me   3
from losing heart: "Do not let terror block
    your purpose. Whatever power he has, he will
    never prevent our climbing down this rock."   6
And then he said: "Accurséd wolf, be still!"
    as he turned to face that bloated countenance.
    "Aim your rage inward and eat up your fill.   9
Not without reason do we now advance
    to the depths. It is willed on high, in the lofty skies
    where Michael avenged the arrogant offense."°   12
As sails that are swollen when the winds arise
    collapse into a heap when the mast is cracked,
    so the cruel beast collapsed before our eyes.   15
Going down to the fourth hollow now, we tracked
    further along that mournful shore where all
    the evil of the universe is sacked.   18

Justice of God above! Who stuffs it full
     with these new pains and punishments? How can
     we let guilt waste us so? As with the pull   21
of waves that swirl above Charybdis,° when
     they crash with counterwaves, forevermore
     these souls must dance their turn and turn again.   24
Now greater than what I had seen before
     were the numbers of the damned on either side,
     chests straining to push great weights, with a mighty roar.   27
They all would come together and collide,
     then each wheeled round and rolled his weight along.
     "Why pinch it?" and "Why throw it away?" they cried.   30
Around the somber circle moved the throng
     till their previous positions were reversed,
     rebuking each other with their scornful song.   33
When each arrived where he had been at first,
     he retraced his semicircle to joust again.
     Feeling as if my heart were about to burst,   36
"Master, who are these people?" I said then.
     "The tonsured ones amassed on our left side,°
     is it possible they all were clergymen?"   39
"When they were in the first life," he replied,
     "because they all had squinting intellects,
     in money matters moderation died.   42
Their howling clearly shows you the effects,
     when they come to the two points of the circle where
     their opposite sins divide them into sects.   45
The ones with heads that lack a hood of hair
     were priests and cardinals and popes. With ease
     avarice finds its full expression there."   48
"Master," I said, "among such souls as these
     must be a few that I would recognize,
     who were all polluted by this same disease."   51
And he: "It would be an empty enterprise.
     The filthy, undiscerning life they led

makes their features indiscernible to our eyes.   54
　　Forever they will collide and crash. These dead
　　　　will leave the grave with fists squeezed rigidly,
　　　　and each of those will rise with a close-cropped head.   57
Wasting and hoarding, they lost eternity
　　　　in the lovely world for this scuffle and this strife.
　　　　This picture needs no prettied words from me.   60
Here you see, my son, the brief ridiculous life
　　　　of those goods in Fortune's keeping, for which the race
　　　　of men compete and squabble and connive.   63
Not all the gold beneath the moon's bright face,
　　　　or that ever was, could bring rest to as much as
　　　　one of the weary spirits in this place."   66
"Of this Fortune, upon whom your discourse touches,
　　　　Master, please tell me more" was my response.
　　　　"Who is she, who has the world's goods in her clutches?"   69
"O foolish creatures, what vast ignorance
　　　　oppresses you," he said. "Let me impart
　　　　my judgment, so you may take it in at once.   72
He whose wisdom transcends all, at the very start
　　　　made the heavens and gave guides to lead them right,
　　　　so that every part would shine to every part,   75
thus equally distributing the light.
　　　　For worldly splendors he likewise put in place
　　　　a general guide and minister who might   78
transfer those empty goods through time and place,
　　　　beyond all human wit to intervene,
　　　　from blood to blood, from one to another race.   81
One state grows fat with power, another grows lean,
　　　　according to her judgments as she deigns,
　　　　which like a snake in the grass cannot be seen.   84
Your knowledge cannot counter her. She reigns,
　　　　providing, judging, making calculations,
　　　　as do the other gods in their domains.   87
No truce may interrupt her permutations.
　　　　Necessity demands that she not pause.

Man's lot is one of constant variations.   90
And this is she whom men put on the cross.
    Even the ones who ought to hold her dear
    revile her name and blame her without cause.   93
But she is blesséd and she does not hear.
    With the other primal creatures happily
    she rejoices in her bliss and turns her sphere.   96
Now we go down to greater misery.
    The stars that rose when I set out for you
    have now begun to sink,° and by decree   99
we must not tarry." We crossed the circle to
    the other shore, above a boiling spring
    that spilled into a ditch it had cut through.   102
Darker than perse was the water. Following
    the downward track where the black current went,
    we found a strange road for our journeying.   105
When this sad stream completes its long descent
    at the base of the malign gray slopes, its path
    ends in the Stygian marsh, where I stared, intent, 108
at the scene before me. In that filthy bath
    was a crowd of muddy people, filling it,
    all naked, all with faces full of wrath.   111
They hit each other with their fists, and hit
    each other with both feet, and chest, and head,
    and chewed each other to pieces bit by bit.   114
"My son, you see now," my good master said,
    "the souls that anger overwhelmed, and I
    would have you know for certain that more dead   117
are down there, underwater, where they sigh
    and make the surface bubble with their breath,
    as you can tell wherever you turn your eye.   120
Set in the slime, they say: 'We were sullen, with
    no pleasure in the sweet, sun-gladdened air,
    carrying in our souls the fumes of sloth.   123
Now we are sullen in this black ooze'—where
    they hymn this in their throats with a gurgling sound

because they cannot form the words down there."   126
Between the marsh and dry shore, we walked round
    the scummy pool, with our eyes turned toward the place
    where the souls were gulping mud, and crossed the ground   129
till we arrived at a tall tower's base.

Canto VIII

Phlegyas; Crossing the Styx; Filippo Argenti; The Gate of Dis

I say, continuing, before our stop
    at the base of that tall tower, our eyes were turned
    to something gleaming at its very top.°   3
There at the summit two small fires burned
    and another signaled back from far away,
    so distant it could barely be discerned.   6
I turned to the sea of all wisdom: "What does it say,
    that flame? And what is meant by the answering light?
    And the ones who lit these fires, who are they?"   9
He said: "What they await is heading right
    across the foul waves already, as you can see
    unless the marsh's fumes hide it from sight."   12
Never did arrow move so rapidly,
    shot whistling through the air from a bowman's string,
    as did a boat that I saw suddenly,   15
coming straight toward where we waited, hastening
    with only a lone rower at the oar,
    who called: "I have you now, accurséd thing!"   18
"Phlegyas, Phlegyas,° I fear this time you roar
    for nothing," my master said. "You have us as long
    as it will take to reach the other shore."   21

Like someone who has heard that a great wrong
    was done to him, and smolders helplessly,
        so Phlegyas glared at us, with all his strong   24
anger held back. My leader instructed me
    to follow him in the boat, and I complied.
        Only when I was aboard did it seem to be   27
carrying weight. When we were both inside,
    the ancient prow moved forward, cutting through
        the water more deeply than when others ride.   30
We slipped through that dead channel. "Who are you,"
    cried a muddy shape that lifted up its head,
        "who come down here before your time is due?"   33
"If I come, it is not to stay here with the dead.
    But who are you, so covered with this mess?"
        "You see that I am one who weeps," he said.   36
And I: "In weeping and in wretchedness
    may you remain, damned soul, for even when
        you are bathed in filth, I know you nonetheless."   39
He stretched his two hands toward the boat just then,
    but my wary master gave him a sharp thrust,
        saying: "Back down with the other dogs again!"   42
Then he put his arms around my neck and kissed
    my face. "Indignant soul," he said to me,
        "the mother who carried you is truly blest!   45
In the world he was arrogant. To his memory
    not a scrap of goodness clings, so his spirit stays
        down in the mire seething furiously.   48
How many who think themselves great kings these days
    will lie like pigs in the muck here, and they will
        leave behind names of horrible dispraise."   51
"Master," I said to him, "while we are still
    on the lake, it would please me greatly if I might
        see him dipped down once more into the swill."   54
And he: "Before the shore has come in sight,
    you will have satisfaction straightaway.

To grant a wish like that is only right."   57
And soon the muddy mob began to flay
    the shade so wildly that for what I saw
    I still give thanks and praise God to this day.   60
"Let's get Filippo Argenti!"° came the raw
    cry of the crowd, and the raging Florentine
    turned his teeth upon himself and began to gnaw.   63
Enough of him. He was no longer seen.
    But my ears were hit with a wave of lamentation
    and I strained my eyes to see what it might mean.   66
Said my guide: "My son, we are nearing the location
    of the city whose name is Dis, inhabited
    by a huge brigade and a somber population."°   69
"Now, master, I can clearly see," I said,
    "there in the valley, all its mosques aglow°
    as if taken from the furnace, fiery red."   72
And he: "They look that way because they show
    the flame that burns inside them eternally
    here in the part of hell that lies below."   75
We had reached the deep moats on the periphery
    of that disconsolate city with its immense
    walls made of iron, as it seemed to me.   78
When we had sailed a broad circumference,
    we came to a place where I heard the boatman shout:
    "Here's the gate! Get out!" Before the battlements   81
more than a thousand of those who had been cast out
    and rained from heaven, looked at us and cried:
    "Who is this man who dares to traipse about   84
through the kingdom of the dead without having died?"
    And my wise master made a sign to say
    that it was his wish to speak with them aside.   87
They tempered their scorn a bit: "Well, come you may,
    but come alone. As for him who has the face
    to breach this kingdom, let him go away.   90
All alone, if he can do it, let him retrace

his fool's road. You'll stay here, you who have been
    his guide on his dark pathway to this place."   93
Reader, decide for yourself if I did not then
    lose heart at what those demons shouted, for
    I thought I would never come back here° again.   96
"O my dear leader, seven times and more,"
    I said, "you have restored my confidence
    and drawn me back from danger. I implore   99
that you not leave me here with no defense.
    And if our going forward is denied,
    then side by side let us go back at once."   102
The lord who had brought me to that place replied:
    "Do not be afraid. No one can interfere
    with our progress, when its warrant is supplied   105
by such a one. You will await me here.
    Let your weary soul be comforted and fed
    with hope. I will not leave you, never fear,   108
alone in the low world." So the sweet father said,
    and I remained in doubt while he walked away,
    with yes and no contending in my head.   111
I could not overhear what he had to say,
    but only a moment seemed to pass before
    they were fighting to get back inside, where they,   114
our enemies, immediately shut the door
    against my master, slamming it in his face.
    Then with slow steps he walked toward me once more.   117
He sighed, with eyes cast down, with every trace
    of self-assertion shriveled from his brow:
    "Who dares deny me sorrow's dwelling place?"   120
And to me: "Though I am vexed, do not allow
    your soul to falter, for I shall win through,
    however they may plot to stop us now.   123
This arrogance of theirs is nothing new.
    It was flaunted once at a less secret gate,°
    unbolted despite all that they could do.   126

You read its deadly inscription. Coming straight
    past it and through the circles without a guide,
      there is one who is on his way to where we wait,   129
by whom the city will be opened wide."

Canto IX

The Furies; The Threat of Medusa; The Angel; Opening of the Gate;
The Sixth Circle: The Heretics

Seeing the color cowardice gave to me,
    painting my face when I saw my guide turn back,
    he repressed his own new color instantly.   3
He stood like someone listening, for lack
    of light enough to let his vision cross
    the thick fog and the air that was nearly black.   6
"Still, we were meant to be victorious,
    or else . . . ," he said. "She promised us such aid!
    How long it seems till someone comes to us."   9
I clearly saw how his last words overlaid
    the first part of his speech, how their intent
    reversed the first impression he had made.   12
But the phrase that he had left unfinished sent
    a new fear through me as my mind supplied
    more dire conclusions than he might have meant.   15
"Does anyone ever come down," I inquired,
    "to this dismal pit from the first circle, where
    the only punishment is hope denied?"   18
"Indeed," he said, "the instances are rare
    that a journey like this one of mine has been

taken by anyone who dwells up there.   21
I myself have come here once before. It was when
    I was conjured by cruel Erichtho,° who designed
    to join souls to their bodies once again.   24
When newly stripped of my flesh, I was assigned
    at her command to breach that wall and bring
    a soul from the place where Judas is confined,°   27
the lowest, darkest, and most distant ring
    from the all-encircling heaven. I know this ground.
    Fear not, I know the road we are following.   30
This powerfully reeking marsh runs all around
    the dolorous city, where we cannot go
    without provoking wrath." I heard the sound   33
of further words, and yet I do not know
    what he said next, because my eyes were steered
    to the summit of the high tower, with its glow,   36
for on that spot had suddenly appeared
    three hellish Furies, who in shape and mien
    resembled women, but they were blood-smeared   39
and girdled with hydras of the deepest green.
    They had horned vipers and small snakes for hair,
    round their fierce temples. Handmaids of the queen   42
of eternal lamentation, all three were
    well known to him who turned and said to me:
    "Behold the ferocious Erinyes up there.   45
That is Megaera on the left, and she
    is Alecto who is wailing on the right.
    The one in the center is Tisiphone."°   48
They were clawing at their breasts with all their might,
    beating themselves and shrieking. I tried to hold
    as close as I could to the poet in my fright.   51
"Now let Medusa° come! He'll be stone cold
    when she gets done!" they cried. "It was a poor
    revenge we took when Theseus was so bold!"°   54
"Turn round and keep your eyes shut tight! Be sure
    that if the Gorgon shows herself to you

and you look at her, you will see the world no more!"   57
So my master cried, and with his own hands too
    he covered my eyes when he had turned me round,
    as if not trusting what my hands could do.   60
O you who have intelligence that is sound,
    look through the veil of these strange lines and see
    to where the hidden doctrine may be found.°   63
Now along the muddy waves there came to me
    a terrifying crash that made the shore
    on either side start shaking violently,   66
like one of those wild winds born with a roar
    when two conflicting heats clash in the air,
    that tears through forests sweeping all before,   69
smashing the branches, stripping the trees bare,
    driving on proudly in a cloud of dust,
    scattering beasts and herdsmen everywhere.   72
My master said, removing the hands still pressed
    around my eyes: "Point the beam of your sight beyond,
    where the fumes from this ancient scum are bitterest." 75
As frogs dart through the water to abscond
    from their enemy the serpent, till they lie
    all huddled at the bottom of the pond,   78
so I saw many wasted souls slip by,
    more than a thousand, fleeing from one who strode
    across the Styx with feet that were still dry.   81
He fanned his left hand often, to clear the load
    of fetid air with which the place was full.
    This was the only weariness he showed.   84
I knew that he had come at heaven's will.
    I turned to my master then, who signified
    that I should bow before him and keep still.   87
With high disdain, he opened the gate wide
    with a little wand he carried in his hand,
    and there was no resistance from inside.   90
"Outcasts of heaven, miserable band,"
    he called to those within from the terrible sill,

"why do you make so insolent a stand?   93
Why are you so recalcitrant toward the will
    that can never be balked, that has added to the weight
    of your pain many times? Have you not had your fill?   96
What do you gain by butting against fate?
    The still-peeled throat and chin of your Cerberus
    should tell you what those who try can anticipate."°   99
He turned away without a word to us.
    Seeming like one who was preoccupied
    much more with other matters than he was   102
with our affairs, he crossed the filthy tide.
    Safe in the holy words and unafraid,
    we approached the city and we went inside.   105
No one opposed the progress that we made.
    I was eager to observe the way things fare
    behind such fortress walls, so my eyes strayed   108
in all directions once I entered there.
    There was an enormous plain, where I could see
    great pain and savage torments everywhere.   111
Just as at Arles, where the Rhône flows sluggishly,
    as at Pola, with Quarnaro lying near
    to hem Italy in and bathe her boundary,   114
where sepulchers make all the ground appear
    uneven, with some lower and some higher,°
    so it was here, but so much harsher here.   117
Surrounded as they were by scattered fire,
    the tombs glowed with a heat much more intense
    than any human purpose could require.   120
Their lids were raised, and from them came laments
    so wretched as to make me realize
    these souls paid horribly for their offense.   123
"Master," I said, "who are these who agonize
    inside the arks, and in voices so abject
    fill up the air with so many doleful sighs?"   126
And he: "The heresiarchs of every sect
    lie here with their followers. Every sepulcher

is packed more fully than you would suspect. 129
They are buried like with like. The temperature
 from tomb to tomb displays great variance."
    He made a turn to the right, and soon we were 132
between the tortures and the battlements.

Canto X

*The Epicureans in the Sepulchers; Farinata; Guelphs
and Ghibellines; Cavalcanti; Guido Cavalcanti Is Evoked;
Knowledge of the Future and the Present by the Damned;
Frederick II*

My master walked a secret path that led
    between the great wall and the agonies
    of the tortured souls. I followed him, and said: 3
"O highest virtue, revolving me as you please
    through all the unholy circles, satisfy
    my wishes now and speak to me of these.   6
Is it possible to see the ones who lie
    in the sepulchers? The lids are raised, I see,
    and nowhere is any watchman standing by."   9
"When they come from Jehoshaphat," he answered me,
    "with the bodies they left above at their demise,
    the tombs will all be sealed eternally.°   12
Here in this section Epicurus lies,°
    surrounded by his followers, all those
    who make the soul die when the body dies.   15
And therefore to the question that you pose
    you will soon have satisfaction, and have it too
    to the other wish that you do not disclose."   18

And I: "I do not hide my heart from you,
    dear guide, except to speak in briefer space,
    as you have inclined me previously to do."   21
"O living Tuscan, speaking with such grace
    and honesty as you go walking here
    in the city of flame, will you please stop in this place?   24
You are a native son, as your speech makes clear,
    of that noble fatherland to which I have done
    much damage, and perhaps was too severe."   27
This sound arising suddenly from one
    of the nearby arks so scared me that I drew
    close to the side of my leader, whereupon   30
he said: "What are you doing? Turn round and view
    Farinata° who has risen now, upright.
    From head to waist he stands in front of you."   33
His gaze and mine already were locked tight.
    He stood with chest thrown out and upturned head
    as if hell itself were contemptible in his sight.   36
By my leader's bold and quick hands I was sped
    between the tombs toward him. "Now you must be
    appropriate in your speech," my master said.   39
When I reached the foot of his tomb, he looked at me
    for just a moment, and then I heard him say,
    as if disdainful, "Who were your family?"   42
And I, since I was eager to obey,
    held nothing back, but told him everything.
    I saw his brows go up a little way,   45
then he said: "They were fierce foes, bedevilling
    my party, my house, and me. But on the attack
    two separate times I sent them scattering."   48
"Though driven out, they managed to come back
    both times from where they were dispersed," I said,
    "an art that those of your kind seem to lack."   51
Beside him rose another of the dead
    just then. This one was on his knees, I thought,
    for all that he was showing was his head.   54

His eyes went all around, as if he sought
    someone else who might be there, but when he knew
    that all his expectation was for naught,   57
he wept, and said: "If high genius lets you through
    to wander this prison where the light has died,
    where is my son? and why is he not with you?"   60
"I have come not of myself. He who stands aside
    leads me through here to one that, it may be,
    your Guido° had disdain for," I replied.   63
His words and the nature of his penalty
    had given his identity away
    and allowed me to respond so thoroughly.   66
He suddenly stood up straight. "What's that you say?
    He 'had'? Is he no longer living then?
    Are his eyes not struck by the sweet light of day?"   69
Noticing how I hesitated when
    he expected me to answer him, he dropped
    down in his tomb and did not rise again.   72
That great soul at whose urging I had stopped,
    who had neither changed his look nor moved his head
    nor turned to watch, once more picked up our cropped   75
discussion where it had been cut, and said:
    "An art they seem to lack? If that is the case,
    I find it more tormenting than this bed.   78
But before the lady who reigns here has her face
    relit another fifty times, you will know
    all about that art and just how much it weighs.°   81
And explain to me, so may you once more go
    to the sweet world, why your people's laws have spurned
    my kind, and why you all despise us so."   84
"The carnage and the savagery that turned
    the Arbia's current crimson," I replied,
    "are the reason for the prayers that we have learned   87
to pray in our temple." He shook his head and sighed:
    "I was not alone in that, and would not have thrown
    in with the rest were it not justified.   90

But there was a time when with open face I alone
    dared defend Florence when the rest agreed
    to raze the city down to the last stone."   93
"And now," I said, "so may peace find your seed,
    I beg you to resolve this knot for me
    so that my understanding may be freed.   96
You seem to know of the things that are yet to be
    delivered by time, if what I hear is right,
    but the present moment, that you cannot see."   99
He said: "We are like those with squinting sight.
    When things are far away, we see them clear.
    The lord supreme still grants us that much light.   102
Our minds are dark when things are close, or here.
    As for the present, we know nothing but
    what we are told about your human sphere.   105
Now, therefore, you may comprehend just what
    our future holds. Our knowledge will go dead
    that moment when the door of time is shut."°   108
It was compunction for my fault that led
    to my next words: "That other shade who fell,
    tell him his son is still alive," I said.   111
"As for why I did not answer him, please tell
    of how my thought was wholly occupied
    in that error you have clarified so well."   114
And now my master called me to his side,
    so to the shade I hastily appealed
    to learn who were there with him, and he replied: 117
"More than a thousand in this part of the field,
    the second Frederick and the Cardinal . . .°
    The names of all the rest I leave concealed."   120
And he hid himself. I turned toward the venerable
    poet my master, thinking anxiously
    about those words that seemed to mean me ill.   123
We moved along, and then he said to me:
    "What has occurred to make you so unnerved?"
    And I satisfied his curiosity.   126

"Let the words that were said against you be preserved
    in memory, but take heed," the sage commanded,
    and then he raised his finger as he observed: 129
"When you stand in her sweet radiance whose splendid
    eyes can see all, then you will learn from her
    the whole journey of your life till it is ended."   132
We turned to the left, from the walled perimeter
    to a central path on which we were to go
    down into a valley. High up as we were,   135
we were sickened by the vile stench from below.

Canto XI

Expositions of the Plan of Hell; Tripartite Division: Incontinence (Outside of the City of Dis), Violence, and Fraud in Lower Hell; Violence Is Punished in Three Concentric Rings of the Seventh Circle; The Deceivers Punished in Ten Concentric Ditches of the Eighth Circle; Traitors in the Ninth Circle; Theory of Art as Work.

At the edge of a high bank formed by a ring
    of enormous broken rocks, we came to a halt
    and looked down on a crueler gathering.   3
Choked by the overpowering assault
    of noxious stink that rose from the deep abyss,
    we drew back to the lid of a large vault   6
on which I saw an inscription that said this:
    "Herein I hold Pope Anastasius, drawn
    by Photinus from the path of righteousness."°   9
"We must tarry here before we can go on,"
    my master said, "till the sense has been resigned
    to the foul breath, and the odor will seem gone."   12
"So the time will not be wasted, can we find
    some compensation?" I inquired of him,
    and he replied: "That is what I have in mind."   15
So he thus began: "My son, inside the rim
    of the rocks, three smaller, narrowing circles lie,

like the ones through which we have already come.   18
All are filled up with damned spirits. So that I
   need only show them to you in due course,
   I will tell you now how they are held and why.   21
The intent of every malice that heaven abhors
   is an injustice, and the result of it
   is to do another harm, by fraud or force.   24
Because only human beings can commit
   a fraud, this is the sin God most resents.
   These sinners endure more pain, in the lower pit.   27
The first circle holds the violent. Since violence
   may have three objects, the circle is split in three
   and has one ring for each kind of offense.   30
To God or self or neighbor one may be
   violent, against his person or possession,
   as I will now unfold it logically.   33
Wounding and death come of violent aggression
   on a neighbor's self. On his property one may bring
   ruin, arson, or extortionate oppression.   36
You will see in separate groups in the first ring
   despoilers, plunderers, murderers, everyone
   who used malicious force on man or thing.   39
To one's own person violence may be done,
   or to one's own goods. To the second ring are sent
   all those who now must uselessly atone   42
for robbing themselves of the world, all those who went
   through their property with dice or dissipation,
   all those who wept when they should have been content.   45
They are violent against God who feel negation
   and blasphemy at heart, who in bitterness
   hate nature and the bounty of creation.   48
And thus the smallest ring with its impress
   seals Sodom and Cahors,° and those who say
   evil of God within the heart's recess.   51
Fraud gnaws at every conscience, and a man may
   use fraud on one who trusts him or one who invests

no special confidence. In the latter way   54
he breaks the natural bond of love that exists
    among all humanity, and thus is sent
    to the second circle, which contains the nests   57
of hypocrites, flatterers, thieves, those who were bent
    on sorcery, simoniacs and cheats,
    swindlers and pimps and all such excrement.   60
But in the former way he violates
    not just this natural love, but what is worse,
    a special bond and the trust that it creates.   63
Thus at the center of the universe
    is the seat of Dis, the smallest circle, where
    all traitors are ravaged by the eternal curse."   66
"Master, your lucid words make me aware,"
    I said, "of how the abyss has been laid out
    and the kinds of people that are kept down there.   69
But those in the thick marsh, those who are driven about
    by the wind, those in the rainfall and its mess,
    and those who crash together and harshly shout,   72
why does the red-hot city not oppress
    those souls with pain, if they have earned God's hate?
    If not, why are they set in such distress?"   75
"Why does your understanding deviate
    so far afield?" he said. "Has your mind been driven
    by stray thoughts into some distracted state?   78
Do you forget the explanation given,
    in the pages of your Ethics,° of the three
    dispositions that offend the will of heaven,   81
incontinence, malice, and mad bestiality?
    How it says there that incontinence will incur
    less blame, offending God less grievously?   84
If you contemplate that saying and you stir
    your wits to recollect the souls you saw
    punished above, just who and what they were,   87
you will see why justice has seen fit to draw
    a line between them and the evil souls below,

why they are less fiercely battered by God's law." 90
"O sun that clears the mists, your answers so
    content me that I am as gratified
    to be perplexed by doubt as I am to know. 93
But please go back," I said, "to where you implied
    that one who practices usury offends
    God's bounty. I would like that knot untied." 96
"Philosophy, to one who comprehends,
    makes clear," he said, "and not only in one part,
    that the course of nature totally depends 99
upon divine intelligence and its art.
    If you read your *Physics*° carefully, then you
    will find, not many pages from the start, 102
that art follows nature, as well as it can do,
    like a pupil with his master. It may be said
    that your art is God's grandchild. It is by these two, 105
as you will recollect from having read
    the beginning of Genesis, that humans were
    enjoined to make their way and earn their bread.° 108
By taking another road, the usurer
    puts his hope elsewhere, and in doing so
    despises nature and her follower. 111
But now come follow me, for I wish to go.
    The Wain has crossed over Caurus the north wind,
    on the horizon the Fish begin to glow, 114
and before us waits the cliff we must descend."°

Canto XII

The Seventh Circle: The Violent; The Minotaur; The First Ring: Violence against Others; The Centaurs; The River of Blood

The place was of an alpine nature where
    we were to go down, a place to be abhorred
    by every eye because of what was there.   3
As with the devastation that was poured
    on the bank of the Adige this side of Trent
    by a quake or by the land's being badly shored,°   6
where down the mountainside the turbulent
    rockslide has formed a pathway to allow
    the traveler to make a rough descent,   9
such was the slope that we had come to now.
    And stretched out near the shattered chasm's edge
    lay the thing that was conceived in the false cow,   12
the infamy of Crete.° Like one whose rage
    is tearing at his insides, he began
    to bite himself at the sight of us. My sage   15
called out to him: "Perhaps you think this man
    is the Duke of Athens, he who struck you dead
    in the world above, coming after you again.   18
Beast, get away from here! He is not led
    by your sister's guidance,° but has come to see

the punishments inflicted on your head."   21
And like a bull that suddenly breaks free
    when it takes its deathblow, and from side to side
    it leaps and wheels, careening crazily,   24
the Minotaur jumped up, and my wary guide
    called out to me: "Run for the opening there
    while his mad fury has him occupied!"   27
We picked our way down the scattered rockpile, where
    the stones beneath my feet were moved about
    by the unaccustomed load I made them bear.   30
I was walking lost in thought, till he spoke out:
    "Are you thinking about this ruin, guarded by
    that beastly wrath I just now put to rout?   33
You should be aware that the other time that I
    delved down into the deep hell's lowest ring,
    this crag had not yet fallen from on high.   36
Not long before he came, by my reckoning,
    who carried off from Dis the great spoils of
    the highest circle through his harrowing,   39
the deep and reeking pit so shook—above,
    below, on every side—that I began
    to think the universe was moved by love,   42
by which, some say, the world has often been
    convulsed to chaos. These ancient rocks, both here
    and elsewhere, all came crashing down just then.°   45
But look to the valley. All who interfere
    with others by violence, doing them injury,
    are boiled in the river of blood that is coming near." 48
O senseless rage and blind cupidity,
    that in the short life stimulate us so
    and in the eternal one drench us wretchedly!   51
I saw a broad ditch bending like a bow,
    just as my guide had said, with its wide embrace
    surrounding the whole plain that lay below.   54
I saw a single file of centaurs race,°
    with arrows armed, between the ditch and hill,

as in the world they had galloped to the chase.   57
When they saw us coming down, they all stood still.
    Selecting arrows, three began to go
    away from the others, approaching us, until   60
one called from afar. "You there! We want to know
    what punishment you are going to," he said.
    "Tell us from there, or else I draw the bow."   63
My master answered: "We will reply instead
    to Chiron° beside you, when we come down there.
    You have always harmed yourself with your hot head."   66
He nudged me. "That is Nessus, who died for the fair
    Deïanira, having managed first to stage
    revenge for himself upon his very slayer.°   69
In the center, gazing at his chest, is sage
    Chiron, who taught Achilles. The other one
    is Pholus,° who was always full of rage.   72
They patrol the ditch in thousands, arrows drawn
    to pierce any spirit who rises from the blood
    higher than guilt allows." Then we moved on,   75
approaching where those nimble creatures stood.
    Chiron took up an arrow, and with its notch
    he brushed his beard aside until his broad   78
mouth was uncovered, and told the others: "Watch
    the one who walks behind. Look, do you see it,
    the way his feet are moving what they touch?   81
I have never seen that done by dead men's feet."
    My good leader, who now stood before his breast,
    that part of him where his two natures meet,   84
replied: "He is alive, as I'll attest.
    Alone I must show him the dark vale, not for my
    or his pleasure, but at necessity's behest.   87
One who was singing alleluia on high
    came where I was, to give me this new command.
    He is no thief, no cutpurse soul am I.   90
But by the power that through so wild a land
    moves all my steps, I ask you now to spare

one who can guide us, a member of your band   93
to walk beside us and to show us where
    the crossing is, and carry him astride,
    for he is no spirit who can fly through air."   96
Chiron told Nessus: "Go then, be their guide,"
    as he turned on his right flank, "and if you see
    another troop, then make them move aside."   99
With our trusty escort we walked the boundary
    of the boiling crimson, where we heard the cries
    of the boiled shades shrieking in their agony.   102
With some, the river rose above their eyes.
    The great centaur said: "These gave themselves to fierce
    plunder and carnage, living to tyrannize.   105
Here they lament their merciless careers.
    Here is Alexander, cruel Dionysius too°
    who gave Sicily so many painful years.   108
This one upon whose head such black hair grew
    is Azzolino,° and that fairhaired one
    is Opizzo d'Esti,° who—and this is true—   111
was extinguished in the world by his stepson."
    I turned to the poet, who told me: "In this sphere
    he leads, I follow. Thus let it be done."   114
We approached a group whose heads and throats were clear
    of the stream. One spirit stood alone, away
    from all of the other ones. As we drew near,   117
the centaur stopped to point to him and say:
    "That one pierced through a heart, in God's own breast,
    that drips blood above the Thames to this very day."°   120
Then I saw some who stood up to the chest
    out of the current, and in this crowd I spied
    many I recognized among the rest.   123
Thus more and more I saw the bloody tide
    recede, till it cooked the feet alone, so low
    that here we went across to the other side.   126
"Just as you see the boiling river grow
    more and more shallow," the centaur said to me,

"here in this part of the plain, I would have you know   129
that on the other side it constantly
      grows deeper till it completes its circle where
      the tyrants are groaning in their misery.   132
Heavenly justice stings Attila° there,
      who was a scourge upon the earth for years,
      and Pyrrhus and Sextus.° And it stings that pair—   135
the one from Corneto, and Pazzo—the two Riniers°
      who turned the public roads to fields of war,
      for the bath unlocks and justice milks their tears."   138
Then he turned round and crossed the ford once more.

Canto XIII

*The Seventh Circle, Second Ring: The Violent against Themselves;
Wood of the Suicides; Pier delle Vigne; The Chase of the
Squanderers; The Anonymous Florentine*

Not yet had Nessus finished crossing there
    when we began to walk into a grim
    forest without a pathway anywhere.   3
Not bright green leaves, but foliage dark and dim,
    not sturdy branches, but each a twisted bough,
    not fruits, but poisoned thorns on every limb.   6
Not even the beasts that hate the lands men plow
    between Corneto and Cécina° can roam
    through such rough, tangled brush as I saw now.   9
This wood is the foul, nesting Harpies' home,
    who drove the Trojans from the Strophades
    with dread predictions of approaching doom.   12
With talons, broad wings, gross feathered paunches, these
    human-faced things sit uttering their lay
    of lamentation in the twisted trees.°   15
"Before going any further on the way,"
    said my good master, "I would have you know
    you are in the second ring, where you will stay   18

till the horrid sand. Look closely as we go.
    Here are things that you would call impossible
    if you had heard me tell you they were so."   21
I could hear wailing, deep and pitiful,
    but there was no one anywhere about,
    and I grew so perplexed that I stood still.   24
I think that he was thinking that I thought
    that all those voices came from people who,
    on seeing us approach, had quickly sought   27
to hide themselves. And so he said: "If you
    break off a little branch, you will soon see
    that what you are thinking will be broken too."   30
Then I reached out, and from a great thorn tree
    I tugged a branch until it snapped apart,
    and the stem cried out: "Why are you tearing me?"   33
Where it was broken, I saw dark blood start.
    "Why are you mangling me?" it cried again.
    "Have you no spirit of pity in your heart?   36
Now we are turned to stumps, but we were men
    when we were on the earth. Truly, your hand
    should show more mercy, even if we had been   39
the souls of serpents." Just as a green brand
    will burn at one end, and the escaping air
    will hiss as sap drips from the other end,   42
so from the stump words mixed with blood flowed where
    I had broken it. I dropped it suddenly,
    and like someone terror-stricken I stood there.   45
"O wounded soul," my sage replied, "if he
    could have believed what previously he had met
    only in the pages of my poetry,°   48
he would not have raised his hand to you, and yet
    the thing was so incredible that I came
    to urge him on, which I myself regret.   51
So that he may make amends, let him know your name,
    that when, as he will be allowed to do,
    he returns to earth, he may refresh your fame."   54

Said the stem: "Allured by such sweet words from you,
  I cannot stay silent. May it not displease
  if I am enticed to speak a word or two.   57
I was the man who carried both the keys
  to Frederick's heart.° I turned them expertly,
  locking, unlocking with such tender ease   60
that scarcely any shared his intimacy.
  True to the glorious office in my care,
  I gave up sleep and my vitality.   63
That whore who never turns aside her stare,°
  keeping her sluttish eyes on Caesar's hall,
  common vice and death of royal courts everywhere, 66
inflamed all minds against me, and they all,
  once so inflamed, then so inflamed Augustus
  that my glad honors turned to mortal gall.   69
My mind, so filled with scorn and with disgust, was
  thinking through death to escape their scorn for me,
  so myself to my just self did great injustice. 72
But I swear by the new and strange roots of this tree
  that I never once betrayed my lord, who so
  deserved all honor and all loyalty.   75
If it is true that one of you will go
  back to earth, restore my memory, which still
  lies fallen from the force of envy's blow."   78
The poet paused for a little while, until
  he said: "Since he is silent, you should start
  to use the time, and ask him what you will." 81
And I replied: "Now you must take my part
  and speak for me. I am unable to,
  with so much pity tearing through my heart." 84
So he began: "That this man may freely do
  what you have begged, then satisfy his mind,
  imprisoned spirit, if it pleases you   87
to tell us how the gnarled wood comes to bind
  the souls, and if you know whether one may be
  set free again once it has been confined."   90

When he had done, the branch puffed mightily
    and then these words were fashioned from that breath:
    "I will briefly answer what you ask of me.   93
When the ferocious soul is finished with
    the flesh from which it rooted itself out,
    Minos sends it to the seventh hole in his wrath.   96
It falls into the forest, blown about
    where fortune flings it. After its descent
    it roots at random. Like spelt it starts to sprout.   99
It grows to a sapling, then to a wild plant.
    The Harpies, feasting on its foliage then,
    both give it pain and give the pain a vent.   102
We will come for our remains like other men,
    but not to wear them. It would not be fit
    that what we steal from ourselves we have again.   105
We will drag our bodies here to this desolate
    forest, where they will hang forevermore,
    each on the tree of the shade that murdered it."   108
We waited, thinking that he might say more,
    but then we were startled by a clamorous sound,
    as when a hunter senses the wild boar   111
and the hounds hot on its heels as they all pound
    toward where he stands in wait, and hears the blare
    of the beasts, and branches crashing all around.   114
And hard upon our left we saw a pair
    of scratched and naked figures running by
    so fast they smashed the tangles everywhere.   117
"Come quickly, death, come quickly!" came the cry
    from the leader. Losing ground, the other one
    called out: "Ah, Lano, your legs were not so spry   120
in the jousting at the Toppo!" Whereupon
    he knotted himself with a bush, as if to hide,
    perhaps because his breath was nearly gone.°   123
A swarm of great black mastiffs in full stride
    filled up the wood behind them, like a pack
    of starving swift greyhounds who have been untied.   126

They reached the bush and fell to the attack.
    They tore the one who crouched there limb from limb,
    then seized the wretched pieces and ran back.   129
My escort took my hand, and I walked with him
    to stand before the torn bush where it bled,
    weeping uselessly through every broken stem.   132
"O Jacopo de Sant'Andrea," it said,
    "you made me your screen, and what good did it do?
    How am I to blame for the evil life you led?"   135
Then my master stood above it. "Who were you,"
    he asked, "who have words and blood now blowing out
    through so many limbs that have been snapped in two?" 138
"O souls who arrived to see this shameful rout,"°
    it told us, "that has ripped the foliage from
    my boughs, please bring the leaves that are strewn about 141
to the foot of this unhappy bush. My home
    was the city that chose the Baptist to replace
    its ancient patron, who for all time to come   144
will therefore use his art to afflict our race.
    And if the Arno bridge did not still contain
    some semblance of his visage at its base,   147
then those who made the city rise again
    out of the ashes left by Attila° when he
    destroyed it would have done their work in vain.   150
I turned my house into my gallows tree."

Canto XIV

*The Seventh Circle, Third Ring: The Violent against God,
Nature, or Art; The Sandy Plain and the Rain of Fire;
Capaneus; The Rivers of Hell; The Old Man of Crete*

By the love of my native land I was bestirred
    to gather up the scattered leaves for him,
    whose voice had grown too feeble to be heard.   3
From there we moved on, coming to the rim
    that marks the second from the third ring, where
    the hand of justice is horrible and grim.   6
To explain these new things, I must now declare
    that we had come upon a plain which would
    permit no plant to root or flower there.   9
The plain is garlanded by the sad wood,
    just as the wood is girded by the band
    of the miserable ditch. We paused, and stood   12
at the very edge. I saw the ground was sand,
    arid and deep, and in its quality
    like that where Cato marched with his command.°   15
O vengeance of God almighty, they should be
    quaking in terror now who read of these
    horrors that were made manifest to me!   18
I saw naked souls bewailing their miseries,

ranged in many herds, and every group seemed bound
    to suffer a separate set of penalties.   21
Some of them lay stretched out along the ground,
    some of them crouched and squatted, and others went
    unendingly meandering around.   24
Those who wandered were the largest complement.
    Fewer in number were the ones who lay
    on the ground, but they were loudest in lament.   27
Enormous flakes of fire made their way
    through the air, falling slowly over the whole expanse,
    like snow in the mountains on a windless day.   30
And just as Alexander° in the intense
    broiling heat of India saw fireballs fall
    to earth, intact, upon his regiments,   33
and had his men begin to trample all
    the soil around them, so as to contain
    the flames while they were separate and small,   36
so I saw now with the everlasting rain.
    Just as flint will kindle tinder, it ignited
    the sand and thus redoubled all the pain.   39
Here, there, the wretched hands danced an excited
    and constant dance as they brushed away the spate
    of fiery flakes that endlessly alighted.   42
I said: "O master, you who eliminate
    all obstacles except that obstinate breed
    of demons at the entrance to the gate,   45
who is that great one° who seems not to heed
    the flame, lying there with a scornful scowl instead,
    who despite the rain remains an unripened seed?"   48
That very shade immediately said,
    knowing he was the one alluded to:
    "What I was when I was alive, I still am, dead!   51
Though Jove wear out his smith, from whom he drew
    the sharpened bolt that on my final day
    was hurled at me in rage and ran me through,   54
though he wear out one by one the whole array

of dark Mongibello's° blacksmiths with the call
    of 'Help me, good Vulcan, help me,' just the way   57
he did at the field of Phlegra,° and then with all
    his might fall down upon me, I guarantee
    that his pleasure in his vengeance will be small."   60
And then my leader spoke more forcefully
    than I had ever heard him speak, and cried:
    "Capaneus, your punishment's intensity   63
grows stronger with your unextinguished pride.
    No torment could be more appropriate
    than your ravings, for the rage you have inside."   66
Then he turned to me, with his face less sternly set.
    "He was one of the seven kings, and with the rest
    besieged Thebes. He held God—and seems to yet—   69
in high disdain, in low esteem at best.
    But his own rantings, as you heard me say,
    are the fittest decorations for his breast.   72
Now follow me, and be careful not to stray
    to the burning sand, but let your feet be led
    close to the forest the entire way."   75
We walked in silence till we reached the bed
    of a stream that spurted from the woods, whose look
    makes me shudder even now, it was so red.   78
Down from the Bulicame° comes a brook
    that the sinful women share, just like the flow
    of this rivulet that through the hot sands took   81
its steady course. Its bed was stone, and so
    were both its banks and both its margins too,
    and I saw that this was the path we were to go.   84
"Of all the things that I have shown to you
    since we crossed the threshold of the wide gate where
    no one is ever stopped from coming through,   87
not one among those marvels can compare
    to this stream that has the power to quench the fire
    that comes raining down upon it through the air."   90
So my leader said, which led me to inquire

if he would have the grace to furnish me
    with the food for which he had furnished the desire.   93
"There is a land in the middle of the sea,
    a wasteland now, called Crete,"° my lord replied,
    "under whose king the world lived virtuously.   96
It has a mountain, Ida, once supplied
    with plants and water bright beneath the sky,
    deserted now like something cast aside.   99
There Rhea hid her son in days gone by,
    concealed in his safe cradle, and had each priest
    make a loud clamor when the child would cry.°   102
In the mountain is a huge old man encased,
    who looks toward Rome as in a looking glass,
    with his back to Damietta in the east.°   105
His head is made of gold of the finest class,
    of purest silver are his arms and breast,
    to where the legs fork he is solid brass.   108
From there he is choice iron, the very best,
    except for his right foot, which is baked clay.
    On this, more than the other, his weight is pressed.   111
All the parts of him except the gold display
    great fissures. Constant tears seep from each crack
    and cut through the floor of the cavern. Slipping away   114
to this valley as they drip from rock to rock,
    they form the Acheron, Styx, and Phlegethon.
    Then they descend along this narrow track   117
till, where no more descending can be done,
    they form Cocytus.° I will not speak to you
    of that pool, which your own eyes will look upon."   120
I asked him then: "And yet, if it is true
    that this stream starts up above, where the living are,
    why does it only now come into view?"   123
"You know," he said, "that the place is circular,
    and going toward the bottom with your feet
    turned always to the left, you have come far,   126
but the whole circle is not yet complete.

So there needn't be such astonishment upon
    your face at every new thing that we meet."   129
And I said: "Master, where are Phlegethon
    and Lethe? You have told me that one is fed
    by this rain, and say nothing of the other one."   132
"All of your questions please me well," he said,
    "but you should find one solution in the roll
    of the stream before you as it boils blood-red.   135
And you will see Lethe too, not in this hole
    but far from here, in the place where spirits go
    to wash when penance has purged guilt from the soul.°   138
It is time for you to leave the wood, and so
    you must follow me closely through the fiery sand
    on the margins, which do not burn, because the flow   141
quenches all the flames above it before they land."

Canto XV

The Sodomites; Brunetto Latini; Other Clerks

Now the solid margin bears us as we go,
　　and the vapor from the stream creates a shade
　　that keeps the flames from the banks and from the flow.　3
As Flemings from Wissant to Bruges, afraid
　　of the rising tide as it rushes in headlong,
　　repel it with the bulwarks they have made,　6
and as the Paduans who live along
　　the Brenta keep their towns and castles free
　　from the Carentana° thaw when the sun grows strong—　9
whoever the master builder here might be,
　　he had made these walls, though not as high or wide,
　　with similar design and artistry.　12
We had moved so far along that, had I tried
　　turning round and looking back where we had been,
　　I could not have seen the forest. Alongside　15
the embankment appeared a group of shades just then,
　　and each one stared at us as they passed by
　　the way that men will stare at other men　18
at nightfall, with the new moon in the sky.
　　Each knit his brows as an old tailor does
　　when he attempts to thread a needle's eye.　21

Looked over by the lot of them, I was
    recognized by one, who reached out suddenly
    and grasped my hem and cried: "How marvelous!"   24
And I, when he held out his arm toward me,
    scanned his scorched visage and began to peer
    at the baked features, till my memory   27
allowed their original image to come clear,
    and then I stretched my hand down toward his face
    and answered: "Ser Brunetto,° are you here?"   30
"Let it not displease you if for a little space
    Brunetto Latini turns back with you, my son,"
    he said, "and lets his band move on apace."   33
"With all my heart," I said, "let it be done,
    or I will sit with you, if you desire,
    if it pleases him with whom I journey on."   36
"My son, if one stops for a second, the laws require
    that he lie for a hundred years on the burning plain,
    forbidden to brush away the falling fire.   39
I will follow at your hem, and then regain
    my company where they wander in their woe,
    loudly bewailing their eternal pain."   42
I did not dare to leave the path and go
    to his level, but like one in reverence
    I walked beside him with my head bowed low.   45
And he began: "What destiny or chance
    brings you down here before your dying day,
    and who points out the road by which you advance?"   48
I said: "In the pleasant life I lost my way
    before the fullness of my age had come.
    It was in a valley that I went astray.   51
Yesterday morning I was fleeing from
    that place when I turned back, and he came to me.
    And now along this path he leads me home."   54
"Follow your star and you will certainly
    come to a glorious harbor, if it is true
    that in the sweet life I had power to see,"   57

he said, "and seeing heaven so kind to you,
    if I had not died so soon, I surely would
    have sustained you in the work you seek to do.   60
But that people of malice and ingratitude
    who came down from Fiesole so long ago,
    though the mountain and the rock still rule their blood,   63
will despise you for your good work—rightly so,
    for it is not fit that the sweet fig should abide
    and bear its fruit where bitter sorb trees grow.   66
A race of envy, avarice, and pride,
    they are blind, as the world has said since olden days.
    Of their customs let yourself be purified.   69
The honors fortune holds for you will raise
    a hunger in both factions for your doom,
    but the grass grows far from where the goat will graze.   72
Let the wild beasts from Fiesole consume
    themselves for fodder, and let them not molest
    that plant—if any bit of it still bloom   75
in their manure—that preserves the best,
    the sacred seed of the Romans who chose to stay
    when the city was turned into corruption's nest."°   78
"If I could have the things for which I pray,"
    I said to him, "then you would not yet be
    banished from our humanity this way.   81
Forever fixed in poignant memory
    is the kind, paternal, loving face I knew
    when in the world above you instructed me   84
from time to time in what a man must do
    to become eternal. I must proclaim with pride,
    for as long as I still live, my debt to you.   87
I will write what you have told of my fortune's tide
    with another text, which a lady° will understand
    and make clear to me, if I ever reach her side.   90
But know this much: as long as I can stand
    upright, with conscience clear, I will undergo
    unafraid whatever Fortune may have planned.   93

This prophecy is not new to me, and so
    let Fortune turn her wheel as she sees fit
    and let the peasant likewise turn his hoe."   96
At these last words my master turned a bit
    round to his right and looked at me and said:
    "He listens well who makes a note of it."   99
I did not give an answer, but instead
    asked Ser Brunetto who were the most renowned
    and the highest born in that circle of the dead.   102
"It is good to learn of some who share this ground,"
    he said, "but the rest require reticence,
    for the time for so much talk cannot be found.   105
In short, they all were men of great eminence,
    all of them clerics and men of letters who
    were one and all befouled by the same offense.   108
Here Priscian° moves amid the wretched crew,
    with Francesco d'Accorso° also among the reviled,
    and had you a taste for mange, you might see too   111
the one whom the servant of servants had exiled
    from the Arno to the Bacchiglione, where
    he left the distended nerves he had defiled.°   114
There is more that I could say, but I do not dare
    speak or stay with you longer, for I see
    a new smoke rising from the sand out there.   117
People are coming with whom I must not be.
    But let my *Treasure*, where I still live on—
    I ask no more—live in your memory."   120
Then he doubled back, like one of those who run
    for the green cloth at Verona, and as my eyes
    followed him, he seemed not to be the one   123
who loses, but the one who wins the prize.°

Canto XVI

The Boundary of the Seventh Circle; Three Florentines;
The Mighty Precipices; The Pilgrim's Girdle; Geryon Appears

In that place to which we had already come,
    the water falling into the next ring
    resounded like a beehive's steady hum,   3
when all at once three shades came hurrying
    across the sand as they broke free from the rest
    of a band beneath the rain's tormenting sting.   6
All three cried out with one voice as they pressed
    toward where we were: "Stop, you who seem to be
    from our wicked land, by the way that you are dressed."   9
Alas, what old and fresh wounds I could see
    burned in their members, etched into their skin.
    Remembering it now still saddens me.   12
My teacher attended to their cries, and then
    turned to me, saying: "Here courtesy is due.
    You must wait, and be respectful to these men.   15
Were it not for all the flames that fly here through
    the nature of this place, then I would feel
    this haste suits them much less than it suits you."   18
They resumed their old refrain as we turned heel
    to wait for them. They reached us, and at once

all three combined themselves into a wheel.   21
As oiled and naked wrestling champions
    circle warily, seeking grip and vantage place
    before the thrusting and the blows commence,   24
so each one fixed his eyes upon my face,
    and his head and feet as he was turning there
    went in opposite directions with each pace.   27
One said: "If our charred faces, singed of hair,
    and the misery of this barren sand compel
    contempt for us and for our every prayer,   30
then let our fame prevail on you to tell
    who you are, who walk with living feet that show
    such confidence upon the floor of hell.   33
This one whose steps I trample must now go
    naked and peeled, but in the days that were
    he was of higher station than you know.   36
The good Gualdrada° was his grandmother.
    He was Guido Guerra.° His good works combined
    the deeds of a counselor and those of a warrior.   39
The other one, who treads the sand behind,
    is Tegghiaio Aldobrandi.° Wise words from him
    the world above would have done well to mind.   42
And I, who am set upon the cross with them,
    was Iacopo Rusticucci.° The savagery
    of my wife did much to bring me where I am."   45
Could I have braved the flames without injury,
    I would have flung myself down from the wall,
    and I think my guide would not have hindered me,   48
but since I would have burnt and baked, the pall
    of fear held back my good will from achieving
    its greedy impulse to embrace them all.   51
Then I began: "It was not contempt, but grieving
    for your eternal misery that lay—
    so heavily it will be a long time leaving—   54
upon my heart when I heard my master say
    respectful words that conveyed the eminence

of the men that we saw hurrying our way. 57
I am from your land. With what fond sentiments
    I have always loved to hear and to retell
    your honored names and high accomplishments. 60
I will leave the gall, to go where sweet fruits dwell,
    as my honest leader promised me, although
    I must first go down to the very core of hell."
"So may your body for a long time go 63
    still guided by your soul," that one replied,
    "so may your fame even afterward still glow, 66
tell us if valor and courtesy abide
    in our city as they did in olden days,
    or if such customs have been cast aside. 69
Guiglielmo Borsiere,° walking in these ways
    of pain as a newcomer to our band,
    has told us things that fill us with malaise." 72
"New people and sudden wealth have brought your land
    so much excess and so much vanity,
    O Florence, the time of weeping is at hand," 75
I cried with my face uplifted. And all three
    took this to be my answer, and began
    exchanging looks that men wear when they see 78
the truth. They said: "If at other times you can
    speak with so little cost and with such flair
    to satisfy others, you are a happy man. 81
And if you escape these dark lands to go where
    you may gaze upon the lovely stars again,
    when you take pleasure in saying 'I was there,' 84
be sure to speak of us to living men."
    And then they broke their circle, whereupon
    they fled on legs that seemed like wings. *Amen* 87
could not be said by the time that they were gone
    from sight, so quickly did they disappear.
    My master thought it best that we move on. 90
I followed, and in a short time we could hear
    the sound of water falling with such force

that, if we spoke, not one word would be clear.   93
As that river (the Acquacheta at its source,
    but at Forlì it leaves that name behind)
    which is the very first to take its course   96
from Monte Viso eastward and to wind
    down the Apennines' left slope to its low bed,
    at floodtide when the waters are combined   99
above San Benedetto dell'Arpe° is sped
    so mightily that it makes one cataract where
    there might otherwise be a thousand rills instead,   102
here too there was such a roaring in the air
    of dark water dropping steeply that the din
    would have hurt our ears if we had lingered there.   105
Wrapped around me was a cord which I had been
    hoping to make good use of previously,
    to catch the leopard with the painted skin.   108
My leader ordered me to work it free.
    I passed the cord from my hand into his
    wound in a coil, and taking it from me   111
he flung it well beyond the precipice
    when he had turned a little to his right,
    and down it fell into the deep abyss.   114
"This strange signal that he follows with his sight,"
    I told myself, "now in response to it
    surely some strange new thing will come to light."   117
How careful men should be with those whose wit
    can see not only what we say and do
    but has the power to pluck the intimate   120
thoughts from our heads! He said: "The thing that you
    are dreaming in your mind, the thing that I
    am looking for, will soon come into view."   123
When the truth he wants to tell has the face of a lie,
    a man should be silent. Though he does no wrong,
    some shame will still attach to him thereby.   126
But, reader, here I cannot hold my tongue.
    By the notes of this very comedy, I swear—

so may the favor that it finds be long—   129
that even those of stoutest heart would stare
   in amazement at the sight that greeted me,
   floating up through the dark and heavy air   132
the way that one who has worked the anchor free
   from a rock or another obstacle will go
   back to the surface, rising through the sea   135
with arms stretched high and feet drawn in below.

Canto XVII

Geryon as Image of Fraud; The Usurers;
Virgil and Dante Descend on Geryon's Back

"Behold the beast with the pointed tail,° who can pass
    over mountains, who breaks walls and weaponry,
    who makes the world a festering morass!"   3
These were the words my master said to me
    while beckoning him to the cliff's edge, near the place
    where the marble pathway ended suddenly.   6
Fraud's filthy image came to us apace,
    beaching head and torso at my master's sign
    but leaving his tail to dangle into space.   9
His face was the face of a just man, so benign
    was the outward aspect that it chose to wear,
    but beneath it his long trunk was serpentine.   12
To the armpits his two paws were thick with hair.
    His breast and back and both sides were arrayed
    with painted knots and ringlets everywhere.   15
Never was cloth that Turks or Tartars made
    so colorful in design and background, nor
    did Arachne ever weave such rich brocade.°   18
The way a boat will lie along the shore
    half in the water and half upon the ground,

the way the beaver settles in for its war   21
in the swilling Germans' land, was the way I found
    that worst of all beasts perched upon the ring
    of rocky ledge by which the sand is bound.   24
The entire length of his tail was quivering
    in the emptiness and lifting its forked end,
    which had its point armed like a scorpion's sting.   27
"And now," my leader told me, "we must bend
    our way a bit so that it will bring us where
    that beast is lying." We started to descend   30
on the right side of the marble path, taking care
    to walk ten steps out on the cliff and be
    clear of the burning sand and the fiery air.   33
When we had reached the creature, I could see
    that some people sat on the sand near the abyss
    a short way off, and my master said to me: 36
"To take the whole experience of this
    circle away with you, you ought to go
    and learn from them what their situation is.   39
Speak to them briefly, and while you are doing so,
    I will see if I can persuade this one to stretch
    his mighty shoulders and carry us below."   42
So I walked on by myself along the ledge
    of the seventh circle and approached that band
    of wretched people sitting near the edge.   45
Their pain was bursting through their eyes. One hand
    or another would fly now here, now there, to stay
    the falling fire or the scorching sand,   48
in the same way that a dog on a summer day,
    with its paws in motion now, and now its snout,
    tries to drive the horseflies, fleas, or flies away.   51
There were none among those people sitting out
    under the flames that I could recognize,
    but each of them had a great purse hung about   54
his neck, and each of them seemed to feast his eyes
    upon the moneybag that he was wearing.

Each one had its own color and device.   57
 The first I saw as I moved among them, staring,
  was a yellow purse with an azure form that would
  have been a lion by its shape and bearing.°   60
Whiter than butter was the goose that stood
  on a sack a little further off, displayed
  against a background that was red as blood.°   63
And one who wore a white purse, which portrayed
  a gross blue sow,° saw me there and raised a cry:
  "Get out of here, whoever you are who've strayed   66
to this ditch! And know, since you have yet to die,
  that my townsman Vitaliano° will appear
  and will sit here at my left side by and by.   69
I am Paduan, and all these others here
  are Florentines who keep shouting, the whole crew,
  'Let him come down, the sovereign cavalier°   72
who will bring the purse with the three goats!'" Then he drew
  his mouth in a grimace and thrust out his tongue
  the way an ox that licks its nose will do.   75
I turned, and spent no further time among
  those weary souls, lest I provoke my guide,
  who had cautioned me that I should not be long.   78
I found that he already was astride
  the savage creature's rump. He said to me:
  "Be bold, and let your soul be fortified.   81
From this point on, our going down will be
  on such stairs. Mount in front, here I will sit
  to keep his tail from doing you injury."   84
As one with quartan draws so near his fit
  that his nails grow pale and shade can make him start
  to tremble at the very sight of it,   87
such terror did those words of his impart.
  But shame, which gives a servant courage when
  he stands before a good lord, reproved my heart.   90
I scaled the hideous shoulders and I began
  to try to say (though my voice did not accord

with my intent): "Be sure you hold me then."   93
But he, who had at other times restored
    my heart through other dangers, gripped me tight
    and steadied me once I had climbed aboard.   96
He said: "Now, Geryon, carry us from this height.
    And, remembering the new burden that you bear,
    make great wide circles and a long, slow flight." 99
As bit by bit a boat backs out from where
    it is moored, just so did Geryon begin
    to move, and when he sensed he was in the air   102
he turned his tail round where his breast had been
    and stretched it out, and it wriggled like an eel,
    and with his paws he gathered the air in.   105
Such fear, I think, did no one ever feel,
    not Phaëthon when he dropped the reins that day
    and burned the sky with a scar still visible,°   108
nor wretched Icarus when he went astray
    and the wax began to melt and his father cried:
    "You are going wrong!" and his feathers fell away.° 111
Not even they could have been as terrified
    as I with nothing but the beast in view
    and nothing but thin air on every side.   114
The wind upon my face and the wind that blew
    from beneath were the only ways I had to know
    that, wheeling, dropping, Geryon slowly flew.   117
And now I heard a horrid roaring grow
    from the whirlpool underneath us, on our right,
    so I stretched out my neck to look below.   120
Then I was filled with even greater fright,
    seeing fires and hearing cries of misery,
    and, trembling in every part, I held on tight.   123
Now for the first time I could really see
    the turn and descent. On every side my eyes
    took in onrushing scenes of agony.   126
As when a falcon for a long time flies
    without catching sight of any bird or lure

("You're already coming down?" the master cries)   129
and, after a hundred weary circles where
      it had taken off so swiftly, comes back down,
      sullen and angry, far from the falconer,   132
so, when we were discharged by Geryon
      at the very base of the jagged cliff, far below
      where we began, he turned and he was gone,   135
vanishing like an arrow from the bow.

Canto XVIII

The Eighth Circle: The Fraudulent; Malebolge;
The First Ditch: Panderers and Seducers;
Caccianemico; The Second Ditch: The Flatterers

In hell there is a region that is known
    as Malebolge.° Like the cliff by which it's sealed,
    it is all made of iron-colored stone.
In the very center of this evil field
    is a deep, wide pit, and in the proper place
    its structure and its use will be revealed.
The belt descending from the high cliff's base
    to the pit is circular. Ten valleys lie
    near the bottom, just above that gaping space.
As the walls of a castle are protected by
    concentric rings of moats, just such a row
    of patterned circles now impressed my eye
as I gazed upon the scene that stretched below,
    and as lines of little bridges will project
    from the walls to the outer bank, here long crags go
through the ditches and embankments to connect
    the cliff to the lip of the pit, which gathers them
    and cuts them off before they intersect.

3

6

9

12

15

18

This is where we were when we were shaken from
    Geryon's back. Now the poet began to stride
    off to the left, and I walked after him.   21
I saw new miseries now on the right side,
    new tortures, new tormentors with long whips,
    with which the ditch was abundantly supplied.   24
The sinners were naked, moving through the depths.
    The nearer file faced us, while the others went
    the same way we did, but with longer steps,   27
just as the Romans, for the management
    of the huge crowds in the Year of Jubilee,
    have a plan by which the opposing rows are sent   30
across the bridge, with one line constantly
    facing the mount, while their opposite numbers wind
    in the direction of Saint Peter's as they see   33
the castle before them.° Here the dark rock was lined
    at stages by horned demons who drove the herd
    of sinners along by lashing them from behind.   36
With the first crack of the whip each one was spurred
    to pick his heels up! No one seemed to care
    to linger for the second or the third.   39
As I walked, one met my eyes with a moment's stare,
    and I said at once when I saw him: "I have not
    always been starved of the sight of that man there." 42
My gentle leader stopped with me on that spot
    and let me go back a bit, with steps that led
    to the one whose face I was trying to make out.   45
The scourged soul sought to hide, with lowered head,
    but it was all in vain for him to try.
    "You there with your eyes upon the ground," I said, 48
"I know you, for unless your features lie,
    Venedico Caccianemico° is your name.
    You are cooked in spicy sauces now, but why?"   51
He said: "I can hear the world from which I came
    in your plain speech, and though I would keep still,
    I feel compelled to answer all the same.   54

I was the one—however they may tell
    the vile tale—who brought Ghisolabella to
    the marchese, so that she might do his will.°   57
I am far from the only Bolognese who
    laments here. There are more of us than they breed
    to say *sipa* from the Sàvena clear through   60
to the Reno.° If it's assurance that you need,
    some token or testimony, just keep clear
    in your mind that we are famous for our greed."   63
And as he spoke, a demon standing near
    lashed him and cried: "Keep moving, panderer!
    There are no women for the coining here!"   66
I soon rejoined my escort, and we were,
    in a few steps, at a place where from the ledge
    a reef was jutting outward like a spur.   69
With easy steps we climbed onto that bridge.
    We left the eternal circlings, and we made
    a turn to the right across the jagged ridge.   72
The ditch was wide to make room for all the flayed.
    My leader said, as we watched them from on high:
    "Stop here and let this opposite parade   75
of misbegotten wretches strike your eye.
    Their faces will be new to you, for they
    were going the same way as you and I."   78
From the old bridge we could see the whole array
    as they came toward us, and like the opposing row
    these spirits were being flogged along their way.   81
Before I had even asked what I wished to know,
    my guide said: "See that great one there, and see
    how he seems to shed no tear for all his woe.   84
His face still wears an air of majesty.
    That is Jason, who purloined the Colchian
    ram through his cunning and his bravery.   87
On his way, he sailed to the isle of Lemnos, when
    the bold and merciless women of that place
    had all laid murderous hands upon their men.   90

There, with love tokens and with words of grace
    he deceived Hypsipyle, the maiden who
    had deceived the other women of her race.   93
He left her pregnant and bereft. Here you
    may see the punishments such vices cause,
    and here Medea has her vengeance too.°   96
All such deceivers move here without pause.
    That is all you need to know of this first ditch
    and of all the souls that are gripped within its jaws."   99
And while he spoke, we came to the point at which
    our narrow path reached the next embankment, where
    it arched once more to form another bridge,   102
over the next pouch. We heard people there
    hitting themselves and uttering loud cries
    and snuffling with their muzzles at the air.   105
From down inside this ditch rank vapors rise
    that cling to the rockface, causing mold to grow,
    and that wage a constant war with nose and eyes.   108
Here the bottom is so deep that we had to go
    up to the bridge's highest point, between
    the embankments, so that we could see below.   111
From that great height we stared down at the scene
    of a swarm of people plunged into a mess
    that looked as if it came from a latrine.   114
My eyes, as they went picking through that press,
    saw one whose head was so besmeared with shit,
    whether he was priest or layman, who could guess?°   117
He called to me: "Your greedy eyeballs sit
    on me more than the other pigs here. Why?"
    And I: "Because, if I remember it   120
rightly, I saw you when your hair was dry,
    and you are Alessio Interminei°
    from Lucca. That is why you caught my eye."   123
Then he began to smack his gourd and say:
    "How have I sunk to this disgusting place
    through the flatteries my ready tongue would spray!"   126

And my leader said: "Now let your vision trace
    a path a little way ahead, then drop
    your eyes till they can clearly see the face   129
of that vile disheveled slut who cannot stop
    scratching herself with her shitty nails as she
    stands up now, and now squats down in the slop.   132
That is Thaïs, the whore. 'Are you greatly pleased with me?'°
    her paramour once asked her, and she stated:
    'Just "greatly"? Why, you please me marvelously!'   135
With that sight, we will let our eyes be sated."

Canto XIX

The Third Ditch: The Sin of Simony; Pope Nicholas III;
Reference to Pope Boniface VIII; Invective against Acts of Simony
and against the Donation of Constantine

O Simon Magus!° and many more besides,
    his wretched followers, who have whored and sold
    the things of God, which ought to be the brides   3
of righteousness, for silver and for gold,
    now must the trumpet sound for you, I say,
    because the third pouch has you in its hold.   6
We had climbed the reef and reached the part that lay
    directly above the middle of the ditch
    containing the next tomb along the way.   9
O highest wisdom, how great your art, with which
    the heavens, the earth, and the evil world resound,
    and how justly does your power deal with each!   12
Along the bottom and the sides I found
    in the livid stone a multiplicity
    of identical holes that were all completely round.   15
By their dimensions they reminded me
    of my San Giovanni. They all were the same size
    as the fonts in that beautiful baptistery,   18
one of which I had to break once, otherwise

someone would have drowned inside it—and here let
    this be the seal to open all men's eyes.°   21
Protruding from each hole there was a set
    of feet, with legs up to the calves in view.
    All the rest was in the hole, pressed into it.   24
The soles of their feet were burning, and their legs flew
    so hard in convulsive thrashings that their throes
    could have broken withes or even ropes in two.   27
On any oily substance fire flows
    along the surface, and here it was the same
    as the flames licked at their feet from heels to toes.   30
"Master," I said, "I would like to know his name
    who is twitching more than any other one
    and whose feet are leeched by a much redder flame."   33
And he: "If you wish, I will carry you down upon
    that sloping bank so you can hear him tell
    who he is and of the evil he has done."   36
And I: "Your pleasure pleases me as well.
    You are my lord, you know that I embrace
    your will, and you know every syllable   39
of what is unsaid." So we approached the place
    where the fourth bank is, moving leftward as we went
    toward the ditch's narrow, perforated base.   42
He held me to his hip in our descent,
    and soon we were standing right before that man
    whose legs were flailing in a fierce lament.   45
"Whoever you are, sad spirit," I began,
    "stuck in like a pole, with the upper part interred
    where the lower end should go, speak if you can."   48
I stood there like a friar who has heard
    the confession of a killer who, placed inside,°
    calls him back so his death may be a bit deferred.   51
"Are you standing up there, Boniface," he cried,
    "are you standing there already? What was stated
    was wrong by several years, and the writ has lied.   54
Have all of your spoils left you so quickly sated?

When you coveted them, you dared use guile to win
    the lovely lady that you lacerated."°   57
I stood like those who think they may have been
    made fools of, not understanding the response
    they have heard, not knowing how they should begin   60
to answer. Virgil said: "You must say at once:
    'I am not who you think I am, I am not he,'"
    and I responded with obedience.   63
At that the spirit's feet thrashed furiously,
    and then he sighed, and in a tearful tone
    he said: "What is it that you want from me?   66
If it means so much to you that for this alone
    you have come down here, to hear what I have to tell,
    then know that the great mantle was my own.°   69
But I was a son of the she-bear, and strove so well
    to advance the cubs that on earth I pocketed
    my spoils, and now I pocket myself in hell.   72
My predecessors are pressed below my head,
    simoniacs all, and all of them flattened through
    the fissures hollowed in the rock's deep bed.   75
When my turn comes I will be flattened too,
    pressed down when he arrives, that other soul
    that I took you for when I started to question you.   78
I have spent more time already in this hole
    with cooked feet, upside down, than he will pass
    stuck here with *his* feet glowing like lumps of coal.   81
A lawless shepherd, his crimes more odious,
    will come from the west, and he will prove indeed
    a proper cover for the two of us,   84
a new Jason, like the one of whom we read
    in Maccabees, whose king showed him deference,
    as to this one France's ruler will pay heed."°   87
I do not know whether in my vehemence
    I grew too bold in the thoughts that I expressed
    in this measure: "Tell me, on what recompense,   90
on how much treasure did our Lord insist

before he placed the keys in Peter's hand?
    'Follow me,' I'm certain, was his sole request.   93
Nor did Peter or the other ones demand
    gold or silver from Matthias° when it befell
    that he took the bad soul's place in their holy band.   96
So stay here in your fitting spot in hell.
    As for those ill-gotten gains that made you bold
    toward Charles, be certain that you guard them well.°   99
And if this intensity were not controlled
    by my deep reverence for the sacred keys
    that in the happy life you used to hold,   102
I would speak in even stronger words than these,
    for your greed, grinding down the good, giving glory to
    the wicked, afflicts the world with its disease.   105
And when the Evangelist had that beast in view
    who sits on the waters whoring wantonly
    with kings, he was thinking of shepherds just like you.   108
She had seven heads when she was born, and she
    drew her strength from the ten horns, but it was gone
    when her spouse lost his delight in purity.°   111
With your gold and silver god, what you have done
    differs from the idolators in this alone:
    you worship a hundred, they worship only one.   114
Ah, Constantine, how much evil seed was sown,
    not with your conversion, but your dowry, which
    the first rich father had from you as his own."°   117
Perhaps it was his rage that made him twitch
    or his conscience, but his two feet kicked like mad
    as I sang these notes to him with a rising pitch.   120
I am sure this pleased my guide, because he had
    a look of satisfaction on his face
    as he listened to the truthful words I said.   123
Thereupon he swept me up in his embrace
    and held me to his breast, and once again
    walked the incline that had brought us to that place.   126
Nor did he tire of holding me. Only when

we stood upon the arch that spanned the fosse
between the fourth and fifth walls, only then   129
did he gently put me down. He was gentle because
the reef was steep and rugged, so much so
that goats would find it difficult to cross.   132
And I saw another valley stretched below.

Canto XX

*The Fourth Ditch: Diviners; Digression on
Manto and Mantua*

In this, the twentieth canto of the first
　　canzone, describing souls submerged by sin,
　　the new punishment I saw must now be versed.　　3
I was leaning forward, ready to look within
　　the depth of the ditch that lay visible to me,
　　whose floor was awash with anguished tears, wherein　　6
I saw a line of spirits silently
　　weeping as they approached us, keeping the slow
　　pace of the living praying a litany.　　9
And as my line of vision dropped below
　　their heads, I saw they were horribly distorted
　　between the chin and where the chest should go.　　12
Each head was turned to the rear, and thus contorted
　　they all were walking backward, bit by bit,
　　for their power to look before them had been thwarted.　　15
Such distortion may have happened in a fit
　　of palsy sometime, but never to my eye,
　　and I put no faith in the likelihood of it.　　18
So may God bestow the fruits of your reading, try
　　to imagine yourself, reader, in my state,

and ask how I could keep my own cheeks dry   21
when confronted close at hand with such a fate,
    our form so twisted that their tears rolled down
    to the cleft where the two buttocks separate.   24
I leaned my face upon the projecting stone
    and let my tears flow down, till my guide said:
    "I see the fools still claim you for their own!   27
Here piety lives when pity is truly dead.
    What is more wicked than spurning God's command
    to heed the promptings of one's heart instead?   30
Look up and see the one for whom the land
    opened up when all the Thebans raised the call:
    'Amphiaraus,° where are you running? Stand   33
and fight the battle with us!' But his fall
    continued till he landed among the shades
    at the feet of Minos, who seizes one and all.   36
He who wished to see too far forward now parades
    backward and looks behind him in damnation,
    making a new chest of his shoulder blades.   39
See Tiresias,° who made an alteration
    of his looks from masculine to feminine,
    and whose members made a similar transformation.   42
When he came upon the coupling snakes, he then
    had to strike them with his staff anew, to obtain
    the plumage of his manhood once again.   45
Backed up to that one's belly in the chain
    is Aruns.° Up in the Luni hills worked by
    the peasants who dwell upon Carrara's plain,   48
he lived in a cave in the marble cliffs, his eye
    delighted by the unobstructed view
    of the sea below and the stars up in the sky.   51
And she whose breasts are turned away from you
    and covered by the long tresses that she wore,
    with all of her hairy parts on that side too,   54
was Manto,° who searched through many lands before

she came to my birthplace. And I wish to say
   some words on this subject for a moment more.   57
After her father the prophet passed away
   and the city of Bacchus fell into slavery,
   she roamed the earth's domains for many a day.   60
Below Tiralli, in lovely Italy
   lies a lake known as Benaco, at the base
   of the Alps that form the border of Germany.   63
The water of a thousand springs that race
   through Val Camonica and Pennino flows
   to Garda, and it gathers in that place.   66
An island sits in the middle. Three bishops, those
   of Brescia, Trent, and Verona, would have the right
   to give the blessing there if they so chose.   69
The low point of the lakeshore is the site
   of striking, strong Peschiera, built to restrain
   the spread of Bergamese and Brescian might.   72
The water Benaco's bosom cannot contain
   is collected at that point and begins to flow
   in a river running down through the green plain.   75
No longer Benaco now, but Mincio
   once the current starts to run, it travels then
   to Govèrnolo,° where it drops into the Po,   78
and soon it spreads into a marsh, and when
   the summer's heat afflicts that level ground
   it is turned into a miserable fen.   81
In passing there, the untamed virgin found
   a stretch of dry land in the marshes where
   no one had farmed and no one was around.   84
She settled with her servants in that bare
   forbidding spot, shunned people while she plied
   her arts, then left her empty body there.   87
The people of those parts, when she had died,
   came together on that ground secure from foes,
   defended by the marsh on every side.   90

There, over those dead bones, the city rose.
    For her who came there first, with no divination
    Mantua was the name the people chose.°   93
At one time it had a larger population,
    till idiot Casalodi fell victim to
    the cunning Pinamonte's calculation.°   96
Therefore, should another story come to you
    concerning my city and its establishment,
    do not let lies devalue what is true."°   99
"Master," I said, "I feel so confident
    in the sureness of your account that, should they try,
    their words would be like coals that have been spent.   102
But speak to me about those who are passing by,
    if any have stories worthy to be heard,
    for my mind goes back to them." And his reply: 105
"Then look upon that one there, with the spreading beard
    from his cheeks to his brown shoulders, for he was
    augur when all the Greek males disappeared,   108
leaving even the cradles empty in the cause.
    He decided with Calchas when the time should be
    to cut the first cable at Aulis. Eurypylus   111
was his name, and in my lofty tragedy
    I sing of him, as you are well aware,
    who know the whole of it so thoroughly.°   114
This other one, with thighs so thin and spare,
    was Michael Scot.° In the tricks of magic fraud
    he was a practitioner beyond compare.   117
See Guido Bonatti. Asdente,° who if he could
    would stick to his last and practice his devotions,
    but repentance comes too late to do him good.   120
See the sad hags who left their threads and notions
    for the false divining of the divine will,
    who cast their spells with poppets and with potions.   123
But let us move along. While we stand still,
    Cain, carrying his thornbush,° casts his light
    where hemispheres meet, on the wave below Seville.   126

The moon was already round and full last night,
        as you must recall, for you came to no harm then
        in the deepest wood, when she was shining bright."   129
So he spoke to me, and we walked on again.

Canto XXI

The Fifth Ditch: Grafters; Malacoda;
The Devil's Wiles

We went from bridge to bridge, exchanging talk
    of which my comedy does not wish to sing,
      and at the highest point we stopped our walk   3
to see the Malebolge's next opening
    and hear the vain cries of the miserable.
      An eerie darkness covered everything.   6
Just as when, flanked by boiling cauldrons full
    of sticky pitch, the worn-out vessels wait
      to be worked on at the Venice Arsenal,   9
since winter means they cannot navigate:
    some make their ships new, some recaulk the bow
      or the ribs of one that has carried many a freight,   12
some hammer at the stern or at the prow,
    and some carve oars, or twist lines, or repair
      the jibs and mainsails—so it was just now,   15
but for the fact there was no fire there.
    Through heavenly art the pitch boiled endlessly
      and spread its gluey coating everywhere.   18
I could see the pitch, but all that was clear to me
    inside it were the bubbles on its tide

as it rose and fell in one great heaving sea.   21
  "Look out, look out!" my leader quickly cried
   and suddenly reached out and pulled me near
   from where I was standing to peer down inside.   24
I turned like one who wants to have a clear
   look at the thing he has been warned to shun,
   who is taken by an overwhelming fear   27
and flees, but looks while he keeps moving on,
   and then I saw a great black demon race
   up the crag behind us, coming at a run.   30
How savage were his bearing and his face!
   With wings spread, what ferocity he showed
   with every step, keeping up his rapid pace,   33
moving lightly on his feet! He bore the load,
   on his high, sharp shoulder, of a sinner's thighs,
   and he gripped the ankle tendons as he strode.   36
He called from our bridge: "Hey, Evilclaws, here's a prize,
   one of Saint Zita's Elders!° Dunk him under,
   while I go back there for some fresh supplies.   39
That town is ripe for plucking, and no wonder.
   Except for our friend Bonturo,° everyone
   is a grafter, changing *no* to *yes* for plunder."   42
He tossed the soul down, turned, and then was gone.
   Never did any hound that has been untied
   move faster after a burglar on the run.   45
The soul resurfaced, showing his backside,
   and the devils beneath the bridge began to crow.
   "This is no place for the Holy Face!"° they cried.   48
"The swimming that you did in the Serchio°
   is not the fashion here. If you don't care
   to be stuck with grappling hooks, then stay below."   51
With a hundred prongs they bit him everywhere.
   "Undercover dancing's what our minions do,"
   they said, "so, if you're able, graft down there."   54
And they did what cooks will set their scullions to
   when with forks they plunge the meat down in the pot

to keep it under so it will cook through.   57
My master said: "It is better that you not
    be seen just now. Screen yourself behind a near
    outcrop of rock and crouch down on the spot.   60
I know the way they do things. Never fear,
    no matter how outrageous their offense,
    for once before I tangled with them here."   63
He crossed the bridgehead and he passed at once
    to the sixth embankment, needing now to be
    steady in manner and in countenance.   66
With all the clamor and the savagery
    of mastiffs rushing a poor mendicant
    who freezes and starts begging instantly,   69
from beneath the little bridge, all at a sprint
    and pointing their hooks at him, came the whole crew,
    but he called out: "There's no need to be violent!   72
Before you grapple me, let one of you
    come forth and hear me out, and then you may
    decide if you still wish to run me through."   75
"Send Wickedtail!" I heard the demons say.
    Then one stepped forward, saying: "I wonder what
    he expects to gain by carrying on this way."   78
"Do you think that you would see me in this spot,"
    my master told the one called Wickedtail,
    "secure so far against each plan and plot,   81
without God's will and a fate that cannot fail?
    So let us pass, for it is heaven's command
    that I lead another on this savage trail."   84
The fiend was so crestfallen that his hand
    let go his grappling hook. "Now let him be,
    let no one strike at him," he told his band.   87
My leader called: "O you who fearfully
    crouch on the bridge, it is safe now to appear
    from the cover of your crag and come to me."   90
I rushed to him, and I began to fear
    whether the fiends would keep the pact they'd made,

from the way they all pressed round and crowded near.   93
Once I had seen a line of troops parade
    out of Caprona° amid their enemies.
    Despite the pledge of truce, they looked afraid.   96
I stood beside my leader and tried to squeeze
    against him, keeping the fiends under close watch,
    for their looks were far from putting me at ease.   99
They aimed their hooks, and one said: "Should I scratch
    his butt for him?" and another one replied:
    "Sure, why not stick it to him in the notch?"   102
But the demon speaking with my leader cried
    aloud as he turned around to face them: "No!
    At ease there, Tangletop, put your hook aside."   105
Then he said to us: "It's impossible to go
    along this crag, for the sixth arch is long gone.
    It's lying in pieces in the pit below.   108
But if it is still your pleasure to go on,
    I know another way that you can take.
    Nearby is a spur that you can cross upon.   111
About five hours from now, it's going to make
    twelve hundred and sixty-six years and one day
    since the road was broken by a mighty quake.°   114
I was about to send a squad that way
    to see if anyone's drying out in the air.
    You'll be safe with them." And then he turned to say: 117
"Step forward, Tramplefrost, and Droopwing there.
    And Baddog, I want you to join the hunt.
    Let Spikebeard lead the ten. And let that pair   120
Lusthoney and Dragonsnout step to the front,
    and Pigface with the tusks, and Scratchbitch too,
    and Littlehoof and crazy Rubicant.   123
Search round the edges of the boiling glue,
    get these two safely to the next precipice
    that bridges all the ditches and runs clear through."   126
"Master," I said, "surely something is amiss.
    Let us go on, just the two of us alone,

    if you know the way. I don't like the looks of this.   129
Where is the caution that you've always shown?
      Do you not see their threatening brows and hear
      their grinding teeth, that may grind me to the bone?"   132
"I would not have you suffer needless fear,"
      he told me. "Let their teeth grind. That is what
      they do to scare the wretches stewing here."   135
They all turned round to face left on the spot,
      first pressing their tongues between their teeth en masse
      to signal their leader, who sounded the charge, but not   138
as you'd think—he made a trumpet of his ass.

Canto XXII

Games of the Devils; Ciampolo's Autobiography;
His Escape; Virgil and Dante Escape

I have seen cavalry break camp and ride out,
    or make assaults or muster on command,
    or retreat to save themselves when put to rout,   3
I have seen coursers dash across your land,
    O Aretines, seen raiding parties there,°
    watched tournaments and jousting near at hand,   6
signaled by ringing bells or trumpets' blare
    or drumbeats, castle signals near and far,
    our own and foreign, sound and sign and flare,   9
but never to a bagpipe so bizarre
    have I seen horsemen move, or infantry,
    or a ship set forth by landmark or by star.   12
We walked with the ten fiends. Savage company,
    but in the church with saints, as people say,
    in the tavern with the drunkards on a spree.   15
The sea of pitch was where my attention lay,
    to learn what the pit was like and to take note
    of the souls inside it as it boiled away.   18
Like dolphins swimming near a ship or boat
    whose arching backs make sailors realize

that they have to act to keep their craft afloat,°   21
from the pitch a sinner's back would sometimes rise
    to ease the pain, then plunge down into it
    faster than lightning streaks across the skies.   24
As frogs with only their muzzles showing sit
    at the water's edge inside a ditch and hide
    their feet and all their bulk, so in the pit   27
I could see surfaced heads on every side,
    but when the souls saw Spikebeard come their way
    they plummeted below the boiling tide.   30
I saw—and my heart still shudders to this day—
    one head still up, as sometimes when you look
    one frog will dive and another one will stay.   33
And Scratchbitch, who was closest to him, took
    the soul by his pitch-soaked hair and hauled him high.
    To me he seemed like an otter on the hook.   36
I was familiar with their names, for I
    had watched them when they were chosen for this run
    and listened to what they called each other by.   39
The godforsaken gang cried out as one:
    "Hey, Rubicant, get out your claws and play,
    and flay his carcass till the skin is gone!"   42
"Master," I said, "I wonder if I may
    learn who he is, this luckless miscreant
    hanging helpless before his enemies this way.   45
Please speak to him." And so my leader went
    to the soul and asked about his origins.
    "I was born in the kingdom of Navarre,° and sent   48
by my mother to serve a lord," he answered, "since
    she had had me by a wastrel, one who threw
    his property and his body to the winds.   51
Then I joined the good King Thibaut's retinue,°
    where I became so skilled a barrator
    that in this heat I'm paying back what's due."   54
Then Pigface, who had tusks just like a boar
    that protruded from his snout on either side,

let him feel the way that one of them ripped and tore.   57
Cruel cats had trapped the mouse. Now Spikebeard cried
    as he ringed his arms around the soul: "Look smart!
    Stand back while I enfork him!" Then to my guide   60
he turned and said: "I think you'd better start
    asking now if there's anything else you want to know,
    before the others tear him all apart."   63
So my leader said: "Among the souls below,
    under the pitch, are there any Italians here?"
    And the soul replied: "Just a little while ago   66
I was with someone from there, or very near.
    I wish I were still hidden where he is,
    then there'd be no hooks or claws for me to fear."   69
Lusthoney yelled: "We've had enough of this!"
    And then he raked the sinner's arm and took
    a sinew out with that vicious hook of his.   72
Now Dragonsnout was gesturing with his hook
    at the sinner's legs, but turning toward his crew
    their captain faced them down with an evil look.   75
As they grew still, my leader turned back to
    the soul, who was staring at his mangled limb,
    and started in to question him anew: 78
"Who was it that you parted from to swim
    to so miserable an outcome on the banks?"
    "Fra Gomita of Gallura.° I was with him,"   81
said the soul, "a receptacle of fraud who ranks
    at the head of the list, a first-class barrator.
    From his master's foes he garnered praise and thanks.   84
As he has said, he took their money for
    a smooth release when he had them in his hand.
    A silky trick, and he had a hundred more.   87
And there's one from Logodoro who's his friend,
    Don Michel Zanche.° Once they start to jaw
    about Sardinia, there isn't any end.   90
How that demon grinds his teeth! They're like a saw!
    I want to go on, but I can't say a word,

I'm afraid he'll scrub my mange and rub me raw!"   93
Littlehoof's eyes were rolling as he was spurred
    by a zeal to strike, but his provost suddenly
    wheeled round and barked: "Get back, you noxious bird!" 96
"If it's Lombards that you'd like to hear or see,
    or Tuscans," the frightened soul began to say,
    "then let me call for them, and here they'll be.   99
Let the Evilclaws drop back a little way,
    so the souls won't fear the things that they might do.
    Just one of me sitting here—and here I'll stay—   102
will make sure that seven souls come out for you
    when I whistle. That's the way we do it when
    any one of us gets free from the hot glue."   105
And Baddog lifted up his muzzle then,
    shook his head, and said: "Don't fall into the snare!
    It's a trick so he can jump back in again."   108
The spirit, who had trickery to spare,
    said: "I must be really tricky then, if I
    am procuring some new pains for my friends down there." 111
Droopwing, against the others, stood idly by
    no longer, but told the soul: "If you make a break,
    I won't come running after you, I'll fly,   114
beating my wings above the boiling lake.
    We'll go hide behind the bank. In any event,
    we'll see how much of a match for us you make."   117
Here, reader, is new sport. The whole complement
    looked off to the ridge, and the first to turn was he
    who had raised his voice the loudest in dissent.   120
The Navarrese had it measured perfectly.
    He planted his feet and broke from the embrace
    of the leader in one leap, and he was free.   123
They all were mortified at their disgrace,
    and most of all the one who had caused the error.
    "You're caught!" he called as he started to give chase, 126
but his flapping wings could not outdistance terror.
    The one dove in and the other had to go

looping swiftly upward as the pitch came nearer, 129
like the angry falcon left with nothing to show
    for his efforts when the wild duck he pursues
    eludes him with a rapid plunge below. 132
Tramplefrost, who was seething at the ruse,
    took wing, but hoped his quarry would abscond
    and provide him with a pretext he could use 135
to pick a fight. With the barrator beyond
    their reach, he turned and dug his claws into
    his fellow demon right above the pond. 138
But the other was a full-fledged hawk who knew
    how to give it back to him, and as they fought
    they dropped right down into the boiling glue. 141
There the heat shocked them apart, but when they sought
    to fly away, their wings were so besmeared,
    as if with lime, that they were truly caught. 144
Lamenting with his fellow fiends, Spikebeard
    sent four of them flying toward the other shore.
    Two landed on each side and quickly steered 147
their hooks above the lake to grapple for
    their limed companions, who'd already been
    baked in their crusts and cooked through to the core. 150
We left them to the mess they were stewing in.

Canto XXIII

The Sixth Ditch: The Hypocrites; Two Evil Friars;
Catalano; Caiaphas

We walked with no companions and no sounds,
    with one before and one behind, the way
    that Friars Minor° do upon their rounds.   3
I was reminded by the demons' fray
    of Aesop's fables, the one in which we see
    the story of the frog and mouse.° I say   6
that *now* is no closer to *immediately*
    than these two cases, if we scrutinize
    beginnings and conclusions carefully.   9
Out of one thought another one will rise,
    and that one bred another one that was
    making my fear grow twice its former size.   12
I thought: They have been tricked because of us,
    so hurt and humiliated that I swear
    by now they must be truly furious,   15
and if their spite is blended with a share
    of anger, they will follow where we've led
    more fiercely than a dog destroys a hare.   18
My scalp already tingled with cold dread
    and my senses fastened on what might appear

behind us at any moment. "Master," I said,   21
"unless you conceal us now, I greatly fear
    the Evilclaws. I know they are in our wake.
    I fear them so, it sounds as if they're here."   24
He said: "Were I leaded glass, I could not take
    your outer form more quickly than I do
    the image that your inward motions make.   27
A moment ago, I felt these thoughts from you
    mingle with mine, the same movement and same face,
    so that I have drawn one counsel from the two.   30
If we follow the right slope down to its base
    we will reach the next ditch, in my expectation,
    and so escape from this imagined chase."   33
He had not finished with his explanation
    when I saw the demons with their wings outspread
    behind us, bent on our annihilation.   36
My leader drew me to him, and he sped
    like a mother wakened by the noise and seeing
    the rising flames as they crackle by her bed   39
and then picking up her child and quickly fleeing
    without stopping even to put on a shift,
    more concerned for his than for her own well-being.   42
Supine, he gave himself up to a swift
    slide on the hard ridge that slopes down below
    to form the outer wall of the next cleft.   45
Never did water make such a rapid flow
    to the bottom of the sluice where it ends its run
    by hitting the paddles to make the millwheel go   48
as my master sledded down the rock upon
    his back, and all the while he clasped me tight,
    not just as a companion, but as a son.   51
As we reached the base, I looked back to the height
    and saw the entire troop of fiends appear,
    but now there was no cause for further fright,   54
for that high providence that placed them here
    to rule the fifth ditch makes them powerless

ever to pass beyond their proper sphere.   57
Below there were painted people in distress,
    weeping, and trudging slowly, with an air
    of great oppression and great weariness.   60
Large cloaks were worn by all the sinners there,
    with cowls that hid their eyes, and cut like those
    that are fashioned for the Cluny monks° to wear.   63
Though the eye was dazzled by these gilded clothes,
    they were lead inside, and sat so heavily
    they made the ones that Frederick would impose   66
seem straw.° A weary cape for eternity!
    Turning left once more, we walked with that parade
    and listened to their moans of misery.   69
The leaden capes with which they were arrayed
    so weighed them down and made their steps so slow,
    we saw new faces with each stride we made.   72
I told my guide: "Please look round as we go,
    to see if there are people anywhere
    of whom, by name or deed, I ought to know."   75
And hearing my Tuscan speech, one trudging there
    cried after us: "Don't go at such great speed,
    you who are hurtling through the dusky air!   78
Perhaps I can provide you what you need."
    My leader said: "Till he overtakes you, stay,
    then match your pace to his, and so proceed."   81
I stopped. There were two whose faces showed that they
    had minds that raced to join me, but they were balked
    by their burden and by the narrowness of the way.   84
They looked at me askance when they had walked
    to where I was, and silently took note.
    Then they turned to one another, and they talked: 87
"He seems alive, from the workings of his throat.
    And if they are dead, by what authority
    are they exempted from the heavy coat?"   90
Then to me: "O Tuscan, who have come to see
    the college of sad hypocrites, we implore

that you not disdain to tell us who you might be."   93
And I: "The great city on fair Arno's shore
    is where I was born and where my youth was spent,
    and I wear the body that I always wore.   96
But who are you, whose misery has sent
    its distillations down along your cheek,
    and why do you wear this glittering punishment?"   99
Then one of the two souls began to speak:
    "The orange cape's thick lead weighs down our frame,
    which is its balance scale, and makes it creak.   102
We were Jolly Friars, and Bolognese. My name
    is Catalano and his is Loderingo.
    Chosen jointly by your city, we became   105
maintainers of the peace, a post for a single
    appointee in most times. How well we tried
    can still be seen in the region of the Gardingo."°   108
"O friars, your wicked—" I started. The rest died
    in my throat as my eye was caught by someone nailed
    right into the ground with three stakes, crucified.   111
He began to writhe when he saw me, and exhaled
    great sighs in his beard. Catalano, carefully
    observing, said: "The one who is impaled   114
advised the Pharisees that it would be
    expedient that one man be made to die
    in order that the people might go free.   117
And just as you see before you, he must lie
    naked and stretched in the middle of the road
    under the weight of each one who passes by.   120
Transfixed with spikes and racked in the same mode,
    his father-in-law lies elsewhere in this fosse,
    and the others of that council, those who sowed   123
so much evil for the Jews."° Seeming at a loss,
    Virgil was staring at the one who lay
    in such vile eternal exile, as on a cross.   126
Then he turned and spoke to the friar: "I hope it may
    not displease you, if the laws down here permit,

    to let us know if there is any way   129
on the right by which we two can leave this pit
    without our having to depend upon
    the black angels to deliver us from it."   132
"Much closer than you hope, making its run
    from the massive outer wall, there is a ridge
    linking all the savage valleys—except this one,   135
where it is broken and there is no bridge,"
    the friar replied, "but you may climb instead
    on the pile of the ruin up to the next ledge."   138
My leader stood for a moment with bowed head,
    then said: "The one who hooks sinners up on that rise
    gave a bad account of this." And the friar said: 141
"In Bologna once, I heard men philosophize
    on the devil's vices, and someone put the case
    that he is a liar, and even the father of lies."   144
A spot of anger darkened my guide's face
    as he strode away, and I no longer stayed
    among those weighted souls, but left that place   147
to follow in the steps his dear feet made.

Canto XXIV

The Seventh Ditch: The Thieves; The Metamorphosis;
Vanni Fucci; Prophecy of Florentine Civil Strife

In that part of the young year when the sun's rays
    are tempered beneath Aquarius, and when
    the nights grow shorter, equaling the days,°   3
and when her white sister's image once again
    appears upon the ground as copied by
    the hoarfrost with her quickly dulling pen,   6
the peasant, with the loss of his supply
    of fodder, goes outside in anxiety
    to see the whitened fields, and smites his thigh   9
and mutters and starts to pace distractedly
    like a wretch whose mind can find no resting place,
    then grows hopeful, going out again, to see   12
how rapidly the world has changed its face,
    and taking staff in hand walks forth once more
    to lead his sheep to graze. Such was my case,   15
because the troubled look my master wore
    distressed me deeply, but he soothed my pain
    when he quickly put the plaster to the sore.   18
At the ruined bridge I saw his face regain,
    when he turned to me, the sweet look I first knew

at the base of the mountain on the desert plain.   21
He looked carefully at the ruin, then he drew
    into himself in silent contemplation,
    and then took hold of me. Like someone who   24
while working keeps a constant calculation
    and thus is able to anticipate,
    he would look ahead and make an estimation   27
as he lifted me from rock to rock, and state:
    "Take hold of this one, but be sure to test
    beforehand whether it will bear your weight."   30
That was no road for anybody dressed
    in a lead cloak. Rock by rock we had to grope,
    he weightless and I half-carried, toward the crest.   33
And happily upon that side the slope
    was shorter than on the other, or else I—
    I cannot speak for him—would have had no hope.   36
All of the rungs of the Malebolge lie
    on an incline toward the deep well's mouth, and so
    one wall is always low and one is high   39
in each of the ten troughs along the row.
    But in the end we made our way to where
    the last rock had broken free and dropped below.   42
My aching lungs had been so milked of air,
    when I finally reached the top, that I had to sit,
    feeling unable to go on from there.   45
"Now you must rouse yourself, for never yet
    has anyone come to fame," my master cried,
    "sitting on cushions or under a coverlet.   48
He who consumes his life, when he has died
    without fame, leaves the world with the impress
    of smoke in the air or foam upon the tide.   51
Rise. Let your soul overcome your breathlessness,
    for, unless the heavy body lets it fail,
    the soul will always prove victorious.   54
There is still a longer ladder we must scale.
    It is not enough to have left the rest, and so

act for your good, if you know what these words entail." 57
Then I stood up and said, with a greater show
    of breath than what I really felt within:
    "I am strong and I am ready. Let us go." 60
So we took up our journey once again.
    The ridge was narrow, difficult, and rough,
    much steeper than the previous one had been. 63
I was talking as I walked, to keep up the bluff
    of vigor, when a voice with little skill
    in forming words came from the nearby trough. 66
Although I had reached the high point of the hill
    made by the arch, I could not tell what was said
    and I sensed the speaker was not standing still. 69
Because of the darkness, even my riveted
    eyes could not see to the bottom of the ring,
    so I said: "Master, let us walk ahead 72
and descend the wall, for I am listening
    without understanding what I hear, and I
    am looking without seeing anything." 75
He said: "A right request should be followed by
    the deed itself without words' embellishment,
    and so the doing is my sole reply." 78
At the end of the bridge, we two made our descent
    to the eighth embankment, and from where we stood
    what was down there in the ditch was evident. 81
In it I saw a horrible multitude
    of serpents, of such weird variety
    that thinking about them now still chills my blood. 84
Let Libya boast no more of phareae
    and jaculi and chelydri in her sands,
    and cenchres with amphisbaena, because she, 87
with all Ethiopia or the Red Sea's lands,°
    has never bred a pestilence of such scope
    or such malignancy. Here naked bands 90
of terrified souls were running, with no hope,
    amid this savage swarm, that they would find

a crevice where they could hide, or a heliotrope.   93
With serpents each one's hands were bound behind,
   and the ends poked through his loins and gathered tight
   in a knot at front, with head and tail entwined.   96
Not far from where we stood, I beheld the sight
   of a serpent darting at a sinner's nape,
   transfixing him where shoulders and neck unite.   99
Never did pen so quickly make the shape
   of an *o* or *i* as he flared and burned before
   he turned to ash and fell into a heap.   102
And when he lay destroyed on the ditch's floor,
   the loose dust gathered by itself and then
   quickly assumed its former shape once more.   105
In such fashion, as affirmed by learned men,
   when its five hundred years are near complete
   the phoenix dies and then is born again.   108
Tears of balsam and of incense are its meat,
   not grass or grain, and when it comes to die
   spikenard and myrrh are its final winding-sheet.   111
Just as when someone falls without knowing why,
   seized by a devil hidden from his eyes
   or a blockage that a man may be stricken by,   114
and looks around him as he starts to rise,
   stunned by the anguish that he undergoes,
   and in his great bewilderment he sighs,   117
such was the soul before us as he rose.
   O power of God, so rigorously applied,
   that in its vengeance showers down such blows!   120
My leader asked who he was, and he replied:
   "Not long ago I was rained from Tuscany
   down to this savage gullet. I enjoyed   123
a beast's, not a man's life, mule that I used to be.
   I am Vanni Fucci,° beast. Pistoia was
   a proper den for an animal like me."   126
I said to my guide: "Tell him not to slip from us,
   and ask what sin has thrown him down here, since

I knew him to be bloody and furious."   129
The soul had heard me, and with no pretense
    fastened on me with his face and with his mind,
    and said, as sad shame colored his countenance: 132
"It pains me more to be caught by you in the bind
    of this misery than it did a short while ago
    to be snatched away from the life I left behind.   135
I cannot deny the thing you wish to know.
    I am this far down because I was the one
    who stole the sacristy's ornaments, although   138
others were wrongly blamed for what I'd done.°
    But lest this sight please you, if you ever do
    escape this land that never sees the sun,   141
open your ears and hear what I'm telling you.
    Pistoia puts out its Blacks, then Florence makes
    its population and its ways anew.   144
Mars goes to Val di Magra, where he takes
    a vapor wrapped in dense clouds, and the might
    of a violent and a bitter tempest breaks   147
on Campo Piceno, where there is a fight
    till the vapor rends the mist above the plain
    all of a sudden, striking every White.   150
And I have told you this to give you pain."°

Canto XXV

The Seventh Ditch, Continued; Cacus;
Infernal Metamorphosis; Puccio Sciancato

When he had finished speaking, the thief threw
    his arms up, making figs with both his hands,
    and shouted: "Take these, God, they're aimed at you!"   3
From that moment on, the serpents were my friends,
    for one approached his neck and circled it,
    as if to tell him "Now your talking ends,"   6
and another retied him with so tight a fit,
    knotting itself in front, that he could not free
    his arms to even wriggle them a bit.   9
Pistoia, Pistoia, why do you not decree
    the flames of your own destruction and downfall,
    since you surpass your seed in villainy?°   12
I saw no soul so proud toward God through all
    the murky rings of hell, not even the one
    who assaulted Thebes and fell from the high wall.°   15
He fled without a word, and on the run
    came a raging centaur who was calling out:
    "Where is he, where's the unripe spirit gone?"   18
I believe not even Maremma° has such a rout
    of snakes as I saw upon him, from the rear

to the part where our human shape begins to sprout.   21
   A dragon with its wings stretched out was here
      across his shoulders, crouched behind his head,
      spitting fire and burning anyone who was near.   24
"That centaur there is Cacus,"° my master said.
      "Below the rock of Mount Avetine, blood flowed
      because of him into frequent lakes of red.   27
And owing to the craftiness he showed
      when he stole the great herd grazing near his den,
      he and his brothers are not on the same road.   30
That brought the end of his crooked dealings when
      Hercules clubbed him down, although he may,
      of a hundred blows, have felt not even ten."   33
While he said these words, the centaur ran away
      and three souls came to stand below us two,
      although neither my guide nor I perceived that they   36
were there until they called out: "Who are you?"
      We stopped what we were saying, and we were
      attentive to them. I couldn't make out who   39
these three might be, but as it will occur
      by chance sometimes, at that moment it occurred
      that one of them had occasion to refer   42
to someone else—"Where's Cianfa?"°—at which I stirred,
      and I placed a finger on my lips to show
      my leader we should watch without a word.   45
Reader, it is no wonder if you are slow
      to credit what comes next, for I was there
      and I hardly can believe that it was so.   48
As I fixed upon those three with a steady stare,
      all at once I saw a six-legged serpent race
      up to one and fasten on him everywhere.   51
Its front feet moved to pin his arms in place,
      its middle feet gripped his belly like a vise
      while it sank its fangs in both sides of his face,   54
and between his legs its tail began to rise
      and it curved up to secure him from behind

after its rear feet spread apart his thighs.   57
Never did any strand of ivy bind
    its clinging roots more closely to a tree
    than the limbs of that disgusting beast entwined   60
round the soul's. The two seemed like hot wax to me
    as their colors mingled and they were stuck tight,
    and neither kept its own identity.   63
In the same way, when a paper is alight,
    ahead of the flame a dark hue starts to spread
    that is not yet black but already no longer white.   66
The other two were watching, and they said:
    "Alas, Agnello,° how fast you are defaced,
    neither two nor one, but something else instead."   69
Where there had been two heads, they were replaced
    by a single one, and in the face it wore
    all the details of their own two were erased.   72
Now two arms sprouted where there had been four,
    and thighs, legs, chests, and bellies mixed and grew
    into members that were never seen before.   75
All of their features had disappeared into
    a perverse thing that was both and neither one,
    that with slow steps went trudging out of view.   78
As across the lane you may see a lizard run
    like a lightning flash as it darts from hedge to hedge
    when the dog days scourge the earth with a burning sun,   81
so I saw a little serpent in a rage,
    as fiery and as black as pepper, bound
    toward the bellies of the two beneath our ledge.   84
Lunging, it bit one where that part is found
    through which we all take in our earliest food,
    and then fell back, stretched out upon the ground.   87
The one it had bitten made no sound. He stood
    gazing and yawning, as if he had been hit
    with a sleepy or a feverish lassitude.   90
The serpent looked at him and he looked at it.
    Thick smoke poured from its mouth, and met and mixed

with smoke from his belly, where the reptile bit.   93
Let Lucan be still, who tells us in his text
    of poor Sabellus and Nasidius,
    and let him wait to hear what is sent forth next.°   96
Let Ovid be still. If he tells how Cadmus was
    made a snake, how Arethusa came to be
    a fountain,° I do not envy him, because   99
in all his transmutations we never see
    two different natures facing one another
    whose forms exchange their substance instantly.   102
The two responded readily to each other,
    so that the serpent split its tail in two
    and the wounded spirit drew his feet together.   105
Then his legs, from thigh to ankle, also drew
    together, and they were joined so seamlessly
    that soon the juncture disappeared from view.   108
The cloven tail took on the anatomy
    the other abandoned, and the serpent's hide
    grew soft as the other's skin grew leathery.   111
I saw the spirit's arms drawn up inside
    at the armpits, while the serpent's short feet surged
    and correspondingly grew long and wide.   114
While its hind feet, which had twisted and converged,
    became the member man hides, from within
    the wretch's member two small feet emerged.   117
As the smoke began to envelop each one in
    a different color and to generate
    on the one the hair it stripped from the other's skin, 120
the one fell down and the other stood up straight.
    Neither turned his pitiless lamps aside, and so
    each watched the other's features modulate   123
to his own. The standing one made its muzzle go
    in toward its temples and made its cheeks express
    ears from the shifted matter's overflow.   126
With what it still retained of that excess,
    in the middle of its face a man's nose grew

and its lips plumped to a human fleshiness.   129
Meanwhile, the one who had fallen started to
 push out a snout and pull his ears inside,
 as a snail when it retracts its horns will do.   132
His tongue, which had been fit for speech and wide,
 now forked. The other's tongue, which had been split,
 became one. And I saw the smoke subside.   135
The new-formed beast went scampering through the pit,
 emitting hissing noises as it fled.
 The other one was spitting after it.   138
He turned his new shoulders toward the third and said:
 "Now I'll let Buoso° have the degradation
 of running on six legs the way I did."   141
Thus the mutation and the transmutation
 in the seventh dump. Put it down to my surprise
 at the strangeness, if I err in my narration.   144
My mind had been bewildered and my eyes
 had been confused, but no matter how furtively
 they fled away, I could clearly recognize   147
Puccio Sciancato.° Of the original three
 he was the only one to undergo
 no transformation. The other one was he   150
on whose account, Gaville,° your tears still flow.

Canto XXVI

The Eighth Ditch: Evil Counselors; Ulysses' Last Journey

Florence, rejoice at how great you have grown,
    beating your wings over land and sea, with fame
    that has spread through hell! I found five of your own   3
among the thieves,° and such to inflict a shame
    that is clinging to me still, and I say to you
    that the fact adds no great honor to your name.   6
But if the things we dream toward dawn are true,°
    then you will feel, in a time that is soon to come,
    what Prato° craves for you, as others do.   9
It were not too soon had it already come.
    I could wish it had, since it must surely be,
    and will grieve me more the older I become.   12
We left that place, going up where previously
    we had descended on the crags we found.
    My leader mounted first, then lifted me.   15
We made our solitary way around
    the rocks and the projections as we went.
    Without the hand, the foot could gain no ground.   18
I lamented then, and once more I lament
    over what I saw, and here I have denied
    my genius its full freedom, to prevent   21

its wandering where virtue does not guide.
    If my good star or an even higher grace
    has given this gift, it should not be misapplied.°   24
In the season when the light-giver turns his face
    the least from us, at the hour when flies yield
    to mosquitoes that have come to take their place,   27
as many as are the fireflies revealed
    to the peasant as he rests upon the height,
    looking down where he harvests grapes and tills the field, 30
with so many flames the eighth pouch was alight,
    as I could see upon arriving where
    the bottom of the ditch came into sight.   33
As the one who was avenged by bears was there
    to see the chariot of Elijah rise
    when the horses strode right up into the air,   36
but found he could not follow it with his eyes,
    seeing nothing but the fire in its glide
    toward heaven like a cloudlet through the skies,°   39
so it was here, where all the fires hide
    their theft, as through the gullet of the ditch
    each steals away with a sinner hidden inside.   42
In my zeal to see, I had risen up on the bridge,
    and had I not grasped a rock, I have no doubt
    that without a push I'd have fallen from the ledge.   45
My leader said, when he saw me leaning out:
    "Inside the fire the spirits are confined.
    With a burning sheet each wraps himself about."   48
"Master, your words confirm what I was inclined
    to assume was so already," I replied,
    "and already I had this question in my mind: 51
Who is in that flame whose top parts so divide
    that it seems to surge up from the funeral pyre
    where Eteocles was laid at his brother's side?"°   54
He answered: "Joined in torment in that fire
    Ulysses and Diomed endure the force
    of vengeance, as they once were joined in ire.   57

There they bemoan the ambush of the horse
    which made the gate that the noble seed of Rome
    passed through as it set forth upon its course,   60
and lament the deceit that took Achilles from
    Deidamía, who mourns him still, though dead.
    And there they pay for the Palladium."°   63
"If they can speak within those sparks," I said,
    "Master, I pray you fervently, and I pray
    that you hear a thousand prayers in this one's stead,   66
that you not deny me my desire to stay
    till that two-pronged flame approaches. You can see
    how eagerly I am leaning out that way."   69
"Your prayer deserves much praise," he said to me,
    "and I accede to it. But you should restrain
    your tongue just now and listen quietly.   72
Leave speech to me. There is no need to explain
    what you wish to know. But since those two were Greek,
    any words from you might be greeted with disdain."   75
The fire came nearer, leaving him to seek
    the appropriate place and moment to pursue
    his purpose. Then I heard my leader speak: 78
"O you who are in one flame and yet are two,
    if I earned merit with you while I drew breath,
    if I earned merit great or small with you   81
when I wrote my lofty verses, then herewith
    remain, and let the one of you tell where
    he went, when he was lost, to find his death."   84
Humming, the greater of the horns that share
    that ancient fire fluttered like a flame
    struggling against a current in the air,   87
and its tip began to wriggle with the same
    undulations as a tongue engaged in speech,
    and a voice was flung from it, and these words came:°   90
"When I was freed at last from Circe's reach,
    who had detained me for a year or more
    near Gaeta, as Aeneas would name that beach,°   93

neither reverence for an aged father, nor
    a son's sweetness, nor the love I should profess
    to Penelope, which she would be happy for,   96
could overcome my ardor to possess
    experience of the world and humanity
    in all its worth and all its wickedness.   99
But I set forth upon the open sea
    with just one vessel from my fleet's remains
    and those few men who had not deserted me.   102
We sailed both shores, Morocco's coast and Spain's.
    As far as to Sardinia did we go,
    and the other islands which that sea contains.   105
My mariners and I were old and slow
    when at last we reached that narrow channel lined
    by Hercules with his marks so men would know   108
that they must not go beyond the bounds assigned.
    On the starboard side Seville now disappeared,
    on the other Ceuta already lay behind.°   111
'Through a hundred thousand dangers we have steered,
    my brothers,' I said, 'to reach these western gates.
    Now has the brief vigil of our senses neared   114
its close, so let us not forswear our fates
    but embrace experience, tracing the sun's route
    to the uninhabited region that awaits.   117
Consider your origins. Living like a brute
    is not the destiny of men like you,
    but knowledge and virtue ever our pursuit.'   120
With these few words of mine, my shipmates grew
    so eager to go on that even I
    could not have stopped them had I wanted to.   123
Setting our stern against the morning sky,
    we turned our oars to wings in our mad flight,
    gaining always on the left as days flew by.°   126
The other pole and all its stars showed night
    their faces now, and so near was our own
    to the ocean's floor that it barely was in sight.°   129

Five times already had the light that shone
 below the moon been lit and then quenched once more
  since we had sailed into the vast unknown,   132
when in the distance on the course we bore
 a huge dark mountain loomed, that seemed to be
  taller than any I had seen before.   135
Our joy was quickly turned to misery
 as a whirlwind rose from the land where we were bound
  and rammed the prow of our vessel violently.   138
With the churning sea it spun the ship around
 three times, and on the fourth time the stern rose,
  as it pleased another, and the prow was downed,   141
and over us we saw the waters close."

Canto XXVII

The Eighth Ditch, Continued: Guido da Montefeltro;
Guido's Evil Advice to Pope Boniface VIII;
Disputation between Saint Francis and the Devil

Its speaking done, the flame stood straight and still,
    and then it went away when allowed to take
    its leave of us through the gentle poet's will.   3
Another one came following in its wake.
    We looked to its tip because of the sputtering
    and garbled noises that we heard it make.   6
And as the Sicilian bull° (whose bellowing
    began with the cries—and this was justified—
    of the artisan whose file had shaped the thing),   9
although it was fashioned out of brass, still cried
    as if transfixed with pain, with a voice that came
    from the victim who was sealed in its inside,   12
with these miserable words it was much the same.
    When at first they found no path or outlet, they
    were translated to the language of the flame.   15
But when at last the sounds had pushed their way
    to the tip of the fire and then forced it through
    the movements the tongue had made, we heard it say: 18
"O you at whom I aim my voice, and who

just now spoke Lombard, for I could discern
    the words 'Now go, I ask no more of you,'   21
perhaps I have come late, but before you turn
    may it not displease you to converse with me.
    It does not displease me, even though I burn!   24
If you have just now left sweet Italy,
    out of which I bring my guilt, and are dropped below
    to this blind world, tell me what there is to see   27
in Romagna: peace or war? I wish to know
    for I come from the mountains between Urbino and
    the chain in which the Tiber starts its flow."°   30
And then my leader, when he saw me stand
    intently forward, touched me on the side
    and said: "You speak to him. He is of your land."   33
I did not delay, but readily replied
    with an answer there was no need to prepare.
    "O spirit down below whom the fires hide,   36
today in your Romagna war is where
    it has always been, in her tyrants' hearts," I said,
    "but when I left, there was no fighting there.   39
Polenta's eagle sits brooding overhead
    at Ravenna, where things are still as they have been,
    and as far as Cervia his wings are spread.°   42
The city that piled up Frenchmen's corpses when
    it resisted the long siege it suffered through
    finds itself beneath the green paws once again.°   45
The mastiffs of Verrucchio, old and new,
    who sank their teeth into Montagna's throat,
    still ply those fangs as they are wont to do.°   48
The white-laired lionet has the towns on both
    the Lamone and the Santerno beneath his sway.
    As summer turns to winter, he turns his coat.°   51
And the city on the Savio lies today
    between tyranny and freedom, as it lies
    between the plain and mountain.° Now I pray   54
to know who you are. Be as free in your replies

as another has been with you, so may your name
    remain forever vivid in men's eyes."   57
After the fire had bellowed in the same
    way as before, its pointed tip went through
    its movements once again, and these words came: 60
"If I thought my answer were to someone who
    might see the world again, then there would be
    no more stirrings of this flame. Since it is true   63
that no one leaves these depths of misery
    alive, from all that I have heard reported,
    I answer you without fear of infamy.°   66
I was a man of arms, and then a corded
    friar, to make amends, and all seemed well
    and would have been, but that my hopes were thwarted 69
by the high priest—may his spirit rot in hell—°
    who pulled me back to those first sins I had known,
    the how and the *why* of which I wish to tell.   72
While I still had the form of flesh and bone
    that my mother gave to me, it was the style
    of the fox, not the lion, that I made my own.   75
All covert ways and every kind of wile
    I mastered, and did such fine things in that art
    that reports went round the earth of my great guile.   78
When I saw myself arriving at that part
    of the life of every man when it is best
    to strike the sails and coil the ropes, my heart   81
was pained by what had pleased it. I confessed,
    repented, and turned friar, and all of these,
    alas, would have secured my interest.   84
Ah, but the prince of the new Pharisees
    was waging war hard by the Lateran.
    Neither Jews nor Saracens were his enemies.   87
His foes were Christians, every single one,
    and none had gone to conquer Acre or
    been a merchant where the sultan's will is done.°   90
He heeded neither the great keys that he bore

nor his holy orders, nor my friar's cord,
    which had made its wearers thin in times before.° 93
As Constantine sent to Soracte and implored
    Sylvester to cure his leprosy,° so I
    had been sent for to be doctor to this lord, 96
for the fever of his pride was burning high.
    He solicited advice from his physician,
    but his words seemed drunken, so I did not reply. 99
Then he said: 'Your heart need harbor no suspicion.
    I absolve you on the spot, so you must state
    how I may cause Penestrino's demolition.° 102
For I can lock and unlock heaven's gate,
    as you know, with these two keys that I display,
    which my predecessor failed to venerate.' 105
These weighty reasons convinced me that to stay
    silent would be the worst response of all,
    so I said: 'Father, since you wash away 108
the sin in which I am about to fall,
    you will hold your throne in triumph if you provide
    long promise, but make the keeping short and small.'° 111
Saint Francis came to get me when I died,°
    but one of the black cherubim came along,
    saying: 'Leave him! He's mine! Justice will be denied 114
if he does not join my miserable throng
    because of the fraudulent counsel he presented.
    I've been at his hair since the instant of that wrong, 117
for no one can be absolved who has not repented,
    and repent what he still wills, no one can do.
    The inherent contradiction must prevent it.' 120
O wretched me! how I shivered when he threw
    his hands upon me, saying: 'Did you fail
    to realize that I know logic too?' 123
He dragged me down to Minos, who wrapped his tail
    eight times round his hard back, and in an excess
    of rage he bit it and began to rail: 126
'This sinner goes to the thieving flames!' And thus

have I come to perdition, robed in the array
　　you see before you, going in bitterness."   129
When he had finished what he had to say,
　　with its pointed tip still twisting to and fro
　　the grieving fire slowly went away.   132
My guide and I walked on from there, to go
　　as far as the bridge the next pouch stretches under.
　　The souls sent here to pay the debt they owe   135
take their burden on by putting things asunder.

Canto XXVIII

The Ninth Ditch: The Schismatics; Mohammed; Fra Dolcino;
Curio; Bertran de Born; The Law of Contrapasso

Even in words not bounded by rhyme's law,
    through many repetitions of the tale,
      how could the blood and wounds that I now saw   3
be fully told? Every tongue would surely fail,
    because our powers of speech and memory
      are not meant to comprehend on such a scale.   6
If all of Apulia's battle dead° could be
    assembled, those of that battered country who
      bewailed blood spilled by Trojan infantry,   9
and those in the long war who fell victim to
    the immense spoils of the rings (so does Livy say
      in his history, where what he tells is true),°   12
and those who felt the heavy blows when they
    resisted Robert Guiscard's° steady press,
      and those whose bones are still piled up today   15
at Ceprano, failed by Apulian faithlessness,°
    and there near Tagliacozzo where the old
      Alardo won the victory weaponless,°   18
and one showed his pierced limb and one made bold
    to display his stumps, it all would not begin

to approach the loathsomeness of the ninth hold.   21
A cask, when its midboard or its cant has been
   removed, is not so open as one I saw
   whose body was split apart right from the chin   24
to the farthole. Down between his legs his raw
   entrails spilled out, with his vitals visible
   and the sorry sack where what goes through the maw   27
is turned to shit. I was looking at him, full
   of awe and wonder, when he saw me stare
   and spread his breast open, saying: "Watch me pull,   30
see mangled Mohammed tear himself!° And there
   walking before me and weeping is Alì,°
   with his face split from his chin right to his hair.   33
And since all of these other sinners that you see
   sowed scandal and schism in their lives, now they
   are ripped apart in reciprocity.   36
Back there a devil waits to hack and flay
   each one of us with the sharp edge of his blade,
   cleaving anew, each time we pass his way,   39
every member of this miserable parade,
   for by the time we have circled the whole pit
   we are healed of the cuts he has already made.   42
But who are you? Are you putting off for a bit,
   by musing upon the bridge, the punishments
   pronounced on you for the sins you must admit?"   45
"Death has not found him," my guide said. "No offense
   brings him here for torment, but in order to
   provide him with a full experience,   48
it is fitting that I, who am dead, conduct him through
   ring after ring of hell, and every word
   is as true as that I am speaking them to you."   51
More than a hundred in the ditch were stirred
   to gape at me, forgetting their agony
   as they stood amazed at what they had just heard.   54
"Tell Fra Dolcino, since you may shortly see
   the sun again, that if he still wants to live

before joining me, he should fill his armory   57
with provisions, lest the grip of snow should give
   to the Novarese a victory that they
   might otherwise find difficult to achieve."°   60
Before Mohammed had turned to me to say
   these words, he had raised his foot into the air,
   and now he put it down and went away.   63
A soul with his throat pierced through was standing there.
   His nose had been cut off to the brows, his head
   had only one ear left. He had stopped to stare,   66
amazed with the rest at what my guide had said.
   Before the others, he stuck his fingers in
   and pulled apart his throat, which was all red,   69
and spoke: "O you who are not condemned by sin,
   and whom I sometimes saw in Italy
   unless there is someone who could be your twin,   72
you know the sweet plain sloping tenderly
   from Vercelli to Marcabò. If you see it again,
   keep Pier da Medicina° in memory.   75
Tell Guido and Angiolello, Fano's best men,
   that if our foresight here is in accord
   with what will be, the time is coming when   78
they'll be bound with weights and then thrown overboard
   near La Cattolica, sunk without a trace
   through the machinations of an evil lord.   81
Neptune has never seen a crime so base
   from Cyprus to the isles that lie near Spain,
   neither by pirates nor the Argive race.   84
That one-eyed traitor, who holds as his domain
   the city from whose sight one at my side
   could wish he had been able to abstain,   87
will call them there to parley, but provide
   such treatment that they will need no vow or prayer
   that Focara's perilous wind be pacified."°   90
I said: "Tell me who he is, and show me where,
   who found the city bitter to his eye,

if you wish me to carry news of you up there."   93
Then he grabbed the jaw of one who stood nearby
    and pulled it so the mouth came open, stating:
    "Here he is, and he doesn't talk. He was forced to fly   96
from Rome, and when he saw Caesar hesitating,
    he extinguished Caesar's doubts. 'A man prepared,'
    he said, 'can only hurt himself by waiting.'"   99
I was shocked to see him looking lost and scared,
    his tongue hacked out right down to his throat's base,
    this Curio whose speech had always dared.°   102
And one with both hands lopped began to raise
    his stumps in the dusky air imploringly
    so that they spattered blood upon his face.   105
He cried: "And Mosca too! Remember me
    who said 'What's done is finished,' the seed that had
    such ill effects for all of Tuscany—"   108
"—and that killed off your whole line,"° I was quick to add,
    at which, piling pain on pain, he turned to go
    like a man that misery has driven mad.   111
I stayed to watch the multitude below
    and saw a sight that I would not have revealed
    without more proof that it was really so,   114
but, knowing that I saw it, I am steeled
    by conscience, a just man's support and stay
    whose sense of right protects him like a shield.   117
Truly I saw, as I can see today,
    a headless body with the others there,
    trudging like them along the dismal way.   120
It held its severed head up by the hair,
    swinging it like a lantern in the night
    as it cried "Oh me!" and caught us with its stare.   123
Out of itself it had made for itself a light.
    They were two in one and one in two. How this
    could be is known to him who in his might   126
ordains it. When he stood right under us,
    beneath the bridge, he held his arm up straight

to bring us closer so we would not miss   129
these words: "Behold my miserable fate.
    Live man among the dead, in your journeying
    try to find another punishment so great.   132
Know I am Bertran de Born, so you may bring
    news of me back with you. I am the one
    who counseled wickedness to the young king.   135
Because of me, the father fought the son.°
    Ahithophel did no worse when he instigated
    wickedly with King David and Absalom.°   138
Two who were one, by me were separated.
    I carry my brain separated from its source
    inside this trunk. In me is demonstrated   141
how the law of retribution takes its course."°

Canto XXIX

The Ninth Ditch, Continued; Geri del Bello; The Tenth Ditch:
Falsifiers; Alchemists; Griffolino; Capocchio

So many souls with wounds so red and raw
    made my besotted eyes desire to stay
      and weep for the mutilation that they saw.   3
"What are you staring at?" I heard Virgil say.
    "Why do you keep your sight so riveted
      on those maimed and miserable shades this way?   6
You have not done that with all the other dead.
    This ring is twenty-two miles around, and so
      keep that in mind if you mean to count each head.   9
The moon is beneath our feet, and we must go.
    Our allotted time grows short, and you will find
      there is more to see than what you see below."   12
"If you had realized why I was so inclined
    to stand and look down there," I told him then,
      "perhaps you would have agreed to stay behind."   15
He had taken up the journey once again,
    and I followed in his footsteps while I made
      my answer, adding: "There, where I have been   18
staring so hard, I believe I saw the shade
    of one of my kinsmen in the crowd that cry

the guilt for which they have so dearly paid."   21
My master said: "Your attention should not lie
    in that direction. Let him stay there, and switch
    your thoughts to other things as we pass by.   24
He was pointing at you as he stood beneath the bridge,
    thrusting his finger threateningly, the one
    called Geri del Bello° by others in the ditch.   27
At that moment you were all intent upon
    the soul that once held Hautefort.° When you came
    to look where he'd been standing, he was gone."   30
"My leader," I said, "his violent death, whose claim
    for vengeance is not yet satisfied by those
    who have been implicated in the shame,   33
made him indignant: I think that is why he chose
    to go away without any word to me,
    and that is why my pity for him grows."   36
We spoke these words as we moved gradually
    to the crag overlooking where the next valley lies,
    right to the bottom, were there light to see.   39
And now, from where we stood upon the rise,
    Malebolge's final cloister was unveiled,
    with its lay brothers visible to our eyes.   42
Weird lamentations, barbed with pity, assailed
    my ears so horribly that my hands flew
    to cover them against the souls that wailed.   45
Such pain as there would be all summer through
    if the sick from Maremma's hospitals, as well
    as those from Sardinia's and Valdichiana's too,°   48
were piled into a single ditch to dwell,
    such pain was here, and all the air was rank
    with putrefaction's flesh-decaying smell.   51
Still turning left, we moved along the flank.
    I saw the depths more clearly as we wound
    our way down to the long reef's final bank.   54
Infallible Justice, God's minister, is found
    meting punishment to the falsifiers there

whose sins she has recorded above ground.   57
I do not believe that it was worse to bear
    the sight of Aegina when all its people fell
    victim to such contagion in the air   60
that along with every other animal
    even the worm succumbed (but the ancient men,
    as the poets who believe the story tell,   63
from the seed of ants sprang into life again)°
    than to see these spirits heaped in disarray
    like sheaves as they languished there in that dark den.   66
One lay on another's belly, and one lay
    across another's shoulders, and one went
    crawling on all fours down the dismal way.   69
With slow steps, without speaking, all intent,
    we watched and heard the sick, who could not put
    themselves upright. Two who were sitting leant   72
against each other, looking, as I thought,
    like two pots set to keep warm side by side,
    and both were marked with scabs from head to foot.   75
I have never seen a currycomb being plied
    by a groom who against his will is still awake
    or a stableboy whose master waits to ride   78
so fiercely as I saw these sinners rake
    their own flesh, because nothing else avails
    against the burning itch. The scabs would flake   81
when they were dragged by the sinners' fingernails,
    the way a knife will scrape a carp or do
    the same to a fish with even larger scales.   84
My leader spoke to one of them: "O you
    whose fingers undo your chain mail bit by bit
    and now and then turn into pincers too,   87
tell us if any Italian sinners sit
    among you, so may your nails be vigorous
    and for the work at hand prove ever fit."   90
"We that you see disfigured, both of us
    are Italian," said the soul, who now began

to weep. "And you, who are so curious?"   93
Said my leader: "I conduct this living man
    ever deeper through the regions of the dead.
    To show him all hell's levels is my plan."   96
They broke their shared support and each turned his head,
    trembling, to look at me. Among the rest
    who had heard the echo of what Virgil said,   99
many did likewise. My good master pressed
    close to me, saying: "Say what you would say,"
    and I began, in accord with his request: 102
"So may the thought of you not fade away,
    up in the first world, from man's memory
    but live instead for many and many a day,   105
tell me who you are and of what ancestry.
    Do not let your hideous penalty and its shame
    keep you from speaking." And one said to me: 108
"Born in Arezzo, I was put to the flame
    at Albero of Siena's will,° although
    why I died is not the reason why I came   111
to this. I told him: 'I can fly, you know,'
    thinking to have myself a bit of fun,
    and he, who was eager but whose wits were slow,   114
demanded that I show him how it was done.
    Because I could not make him Dedalus,
    he had me burned by one who called him son.   117
What brought me to this tenth and last pit was
    alchemy. Minos damned me to this place,
    whose judgment cannot be erroneous."   120
To the poet I said: "Has there ever been a race
    so empty-headed as the Sienese?
    They're far worse than the French, in any case."   123
The other leper, listening to these
    remarks of mine, responded: "Even so,
    you must make an exception for Stricca, if you please, 126
that moderate spender, and for Niccolò,
    who showed how clove and costliness could sit

together in the garden where such seeds grow,   129
and that club where Caccia d'Asciano once saw fit
    to squander his vineyard and his woodland too
    and Meo the pixilated showed his wit.°   132
But let your eye grow sharp to show you who
    seconds you on Sienese stupidity,
    so that my face may also answer you.   135
I am Capocchio's shade.° Through alchemy
    I gave the metals a deceptive shape.
    And you, if I have eyed you properly,   138
will recall how skilled I was as nature's ape."

Canto XXX

The Tenth Ditch, Continued: Impersonators;
Gianni Schicchi; Myrrha; Counterfeiters: Master Adam;
False Witnesses: Sinon; Potiphar's Wife

In days when Juno burned with indignation
    at the Theban blood because of Semelè,
      showing her wrath on more than one occasion,   3
Athamas suffered such insanity
    that when he saw his wife, who was holding one
      of their sons in each arm, he cried violently: 6
"See the lioness and her cubs! Before they run
    to the pass, spread out the nets along the ground!"
      And then with ruthless claws he seized his son   9
Learchus and began to whirl him round
    and smashed him on a rock. She, horrified,
      leaped in the sea with her other charge and drowned.°   12
When Fortune leveled the all-daring pride
    of the Trojans by inflicting the long war
      in which the king and all his kingdom died,   15
Hecuba, lost, enslaved, her heart made sore
    to see Polyxena dead and then to find
      her Polydorus stretched upon the shore,   18
was driven to such madness that she declined

to howling and barking like a dog because
    the weight of the great grief had so wrenched her mind.°   21
But frenzy never showed so furious
    a face in Thebes or Troy, inciting men
    or beasts with such ferocity as was   24
shown by two souls that came running up just then,
    naked and pale, biting everything around
    like pigs that have been turned out of the pen.   27
Sinking its tusks into his nape, one downed
    Capocchio and dragged him on ahead
    so that his belly scraped the solid ground.   30
"That lunatic is Gianni Schicchi,"° said
    the Aretine, who was shivering with fear.
    "Like a rabid dog he rips the other dead."   33
"So may its fangs not find you, please make clear,"
    I said to him, "who the other one may be
    before it turns and runs away from here."   36
"That is the ancient shade," he answered me,
    "of wicked Myrrha, who came to love her father
    beyond the bounds of all propriety.°   39
She counterfeited the image of another
    so she might dare to lie with him in sin,
    much like the demon running off, that other   42
who counterfeited Buoso Donati to win
    the lady of the herd, and even made
    a will with the proper language all put in."   45
When those rabid two on whom my eyes had stayed
    were gone at last, I turned round to survey
    the ranks of many a misbegotten shade.   48
There was one shaped like a lute, so I would say,
    if the part below the groin where man is split,
    forking in two, had here been cut away.   51
Because of the dropsy, in which the humors sit
    so ill-mixed that the members are badly blended,
    with face and belly disproportionate,   54
his lips spread like a hectic's when distended

by racking thirst, with both of them thrusting out,
    one curling up while the other one descended.   57
"O you who are here in this horrid world without
    any punishment," he said, "though I cannot see
    just why that is, behold me and take note   60
of Master Adam° in his misery.
    Alive I had everything I wished, and here
    one drop of water would be all to me.   63
The streams of Casentino, cool and clear,
    flowing softly from the green hills as they race
    down to the Arno, constantly appear   66
before me, and not vainly, in this place.
    The image of them parches me much more
    than this disease that wastes away my face.   69
The rigid justice prodding at my core
    uses the place where I misused my wit
    and makes my sighs fly faster than before.   72
Romena is there, where I learned to counterfeit
    the coins stamped with the Baptist, and was thrown
    on the flames and burnt alive because of it.   75
I would rather see one of those brothers moan—
    Alessandro, Guido, the other one—at my side
    than have the Fonte Branda for my own.   78
If the rabid souls who run around have not lied,
    one of the three is already here below.
    What good is that to me, whose limbs are tied?   81
Were I still light enough that I could go,
    every hundred years, one inch along the ground,
    I would have set out already, even though   84
this circle is eleven miles around
    and half a mile across, to find that man
    down here where the disfigured ones abound.   87
Because of them I am numbered in this clan.
    The striking of the florins with the three
    carats of alloy—it was all their plan."   90
I said: "And who might these two wretches be,

steaming like wet hands in the winter chill,
    lying close by your western boundary?"   93
And he: "I found them there, completely still,
    when I was first rained down into this trench.
    They have never moved, and I think they never will.   96
Joseph's accuser is that lying wench,°
    and this is Sinon, Troy's false Greek.° The drought
    of fever makes them give off such a stench."   99
And perhaps annoyed at being talked about
    with such dark insinuation, one of them
    punched him right where his solid paunch puffed out.   102
It sounded like the beating of a drum.
    Then Master Adam smacked him in the face
    with an arm that was just as hard, and said to him: 105
"My limbs may keep me fastened to this place
    because they are so heavy, but at my side
    I have a free arm fit for such a case."   108
"When you were burned," the other one replied,
    "there wasn't very much that arm could do,
    but it worked just fine for the coins you falsified."   111
And the dropsical: "What you're saying now is true,
    but you didn't give such truthful testimony
    the day the Trojan leaders questioned you."   114
"My words were false. You falsified the money,"
    said Sinon. "One sin brought me here. Yours were
    a multitude. What demon did so many?"   117
And the paunch: "Recall the horse, you perjurer.
    May it stretch you on the rack to realize
    the whole world knows you for a lying cur."   120
"May you be racked by the thirst that cracks and dries
    your tongue," the Greek said, "and the rancid fen
    that makes your gut a hedge before your eyes."   123
"Your sickness spreads your big mouth, which has been
    your bane before," said the coiner. "I am sick
    with thirst, and humors make me swell, but then   126
your head aches and your limbs burn. You'd be quick

to give, without much need for an invitation,
    the mirror of Narcissus a good lick."°   129
I was following this with all my concentration
    when my master told me: "Watch some more, I say,
    and then you will answer to my indignation."   132
And when I heard him speak to me that way
    in anger, I turned to face him hurriedly
    with a shame that shakes me to this very day.   135
As one who dreams he is in jeopardy
    and, dreaming, wishes it were a dream, and thus
    wants what is real as if it were fantasy,   138
so I became, all speechless there, because
    I wanted to seek pardon, and I did
    seek pardon without knowing that I was.   141
"Less shame would wash away," my master said,
    "a greater fault than yours, so do not fear,
    and let your sadness dissipate. Instead,   144
remember that I always will be near
    if it ever should befall that fortune brings
    such arguments as this one to your ear,   147
for it is low to want to hear such things."

Canto XXXI

*The Giants (Nimrod, Ephialtes, Briareus, and Antaeus);
Descent to Cocytus*

I had been pricked by one and the same tongue,
    making my two cheeks tingle and turn red,
    which then supplied the balm where it had stung.   3
In much the same way, I have heard it said,
    where the spear of Achilles and his father hit
    came a sad gift, then a good one in its stead.°   6
We turned our backs upon the dreadful pit
    and then without a word we climbed the height
    of the embankment that surrounded it.   9
Here it was less than day and less than night.
    I could hardly see ahead as we went on,
    but then I heard a horn blast with such might   12
that thunder is quiet in comparison.
    My eyes were drawn to one spot as I traced
    the sound right back to where it had begun.   15
Not even Roland blew so fiercely,° faced
    with the dolorous rout of Charlemagne's brigade
    when the ranks of the holy guardsmen were laid waste.   18
And shortly after I had turned my head
    to look that way, I saw what seemed to be

a host of enormous towers, so I said: 21
"Master, what is that city there?" And he:
  "You pierce the darkness from too far, and stray
  in your imaginings of what you see.   24
When you are near, your vision will display
  how distance makes the sense misunderstand,
  so spur your footsteps on along the way."   27
Then, as he took me lovingly by the hand:
  "Lest the strangeness overwhelm you, you should know
  before we cross the intervening land   30
that those are giants, not towers, where we must go,
  and from the waist down they are standing where
  the bank surrounds them, in the pit below."   33
As when a mist whose vapor packs the air
  begins to dissipate, and bit by bit
  the eye makes out more clearly what is there,   36
as I came nearer and nearer to the pit,
  cutting the dark and thick air with my sight,
  my error fled and fear succeeded it.   39
For just as Montereggione° crowns the height
  of its long round wall with towers in the sky,
  so here the horrible giants, whom Jove's might   42
still threatens when he thunders from on high,°
  betowered with half themselves the bank that drew
  a circle round the pit. Already I   45
saw the face of one of them come into view,
  his dangling arms, his shoulders and his chest,
  and the upper portion of his belly too.   48
Nature, when she decided to desist
  from making them, and took such instruments
  away from Mars, was acting for the best.   51
Although she does not repent of elephants
  and whales, those who consider it will find
  that she demonstrates more justice and good sense,   54
for if she added faculty of mind
  to power and malevolence, our race

would be helpless against creatures of such kind.   57
His face was as big as the pinecone Rome displays
    before Saint Peter's on the holy ground,°
    and his bones were in proportion to his face.   60
The bank, which was an apron all around
    his lower parts, revealed his upper shape
    and length, so that three Frieslanders° would sound   63
an empty boast if they thought to reach his nape,
    for I noted thirty spans° of him, or more,
    downward from where a man will tie his cape.   66
"Raphèl maì amècche zabì almi!" tore°
    from his raw throat, and that fierce cry seemed to be
    the sweetest psalm his mouth was fitted for.   69
And then my leader: "Mass of stupidity,
    keep to your horn for venting your frustration
    when these rages come upon you suddenly!   72
Tower of confusion, make an examination
    of your own neck till you find the strap you wear
    that holds it on your huge chest like a decoration."   75
Then he said to me: "That self-accuser there
    is Nimrod. Through his evil thought alone
    there is not one common language everywhere.°   78
Let us not waste breath, but leave him on his own.
    All languages will sound to him as will
    his tongue to us, which is totally unknown."   81
Then, turning to the left, we walked until
    we had gone as far as a crossbow shot and found
    the next one, far more fierce and huger still.   84
Just who the master was who had him bound
    I cannot say, but he was shackled tight
    by a chain that ringed his neck and wrapped around   87
to pin his left arm before him and his right
    behind his back, then coiled five times before
    it wound below his waist and out of sight.   90
"This proud one tried his strength by making war
    upon almighty Jove," said my leader then,

"and here you see the fruit his efforts bore.   93
    He, Ephialtes, struck the great blows° when
    giants made gods afraid. Then they swung free,
    those arms of his, but they did not move again."   96
And then I said to him: "If it could be,
    these eyes of mine would wish to gaze upon
    Briareus in his immensity."°   99
"You will see Antaeus° not much further on,
    who can speak and who is also unrestrained.
    He will set us down where the guiltiest have gone.   102
The one you want is far off," he explained.
    "Though his face is more ferocious, his limbs take
    the shape of this one's, and he too is chained."   105
Never did nature cause the earth to quake
    and make a tower tremble with such might
    as when Ephialtes now began to shake.   108
Now more than ever, death filled me with fright,
    and the fear alone would have furnished the event
    had I not seen the chains that held him tight.   111
Then we came upon Antaeus as we went.
    He rose a full five ells above the ground,
    with his head not counted in the measurement.   114
"O you who, in the fateful vale that crowned
    Scipio heir of glory on the day
    when Hannibal and his army turned around,°   117
once took a thousand lions as your prey,
    through whom, had you joined your brothers in the field
    in their high war, there are many who still say   120
that the sons of earth would have forced the gods to yield,
    now lower us, not disdaining to do so,
    to the cold in which Cocytus° has been sealed.   123
Do not curl your lip, but bend. Do not make us go
    to Tityus or Typhon.° Be assured
    this man can give what is longed for here below.   126
Through him your earthly fame may be restored,
    for he lives, and expects a long life, unless graced

by an early summons to his last reward." 129
So spoke my master. The other one in haste
    held out the huge hands in whose vigorous
    clutches had Hercules once been embraced. 132
When Virgil felt their grip, he called me thus:
    "Come here to me, so I may gather you,"
    and made one bundle of the two of us. 135
As the Garisenda° seems to someone who
    stands under it when a cloud comes overhead
    athwart the way the tower leans, so too 138
Antaeus seemed as he stooped with his hands spread
    to pick me up. Just then I wished we were
    descending by another road instead. 141
Where the bottom swallows Judas and Lucifer
    he set us down, and waited not at all,
    but as soon as we were clear began to stir 144
and like a ship's mast rose up straight and tall.

Canto XXXII

*The Ninth and Last Circle: The Treacherous Freezing
in Cocytus; The First Ring of the Traitors: Caïna
(Traitors to Kindred); The Second Ring: Antenora
(Traitors to Country or Faction)*

With harsh and clacking rhymes that could convey
    the nature of that hole of misery
    on which all other rocks converge and weigh,   3
I would press out the juice more thoroughly
    from my conception. Lacking them, I fall
    to the work at hand with some anxiety.   6
To try to describe the very floor of all
    the universe is nothing to attract
    an idle mind, no task for tongues that call   9
to mama and papa. May my attempts be backed
    by those ladies that inspired Amphion° when
    he walled Thebes, that my words may hold the fact.   12
O most misbegotten rabble in that den
    so hard to speak of, better far had you
    been born as sheep or goats instead of men!   15
Down in the dark pit we'd been carried to,
    far beneath the giant's feet, I was standing where
    I had the enormous wall still fixed in view   18

when I heard a voice that said to me: "Take care
    not to step upon the poor heads, as you pass,
    of the weary brothers who are lying there."   21
Then I saw around me, under me, a mass
    of solid water, a lake so frozen over
    that it looked much less like water than like glass.   24
Never in Austria did the Danube river
    or the distant Don, where winter is most bleak,
    provide their currents with so thick a cover   27
as there was here, and if the entire peak
    of Tambernic or Pietrapana° were
    to fall on it, not even the edge would creak.   30
As when the croaking frogs will barely stir,
    with mouths out of water, while the peasant will
    dream of the gleaning that means so much to her,   33
so the dolorous souls in the ice were livid till
    their heads emerged with faces shame had dyed.
    Their teeth were clicking like the stork's long bill.   36
Each face looked down. Their mouths all testified
    to the bitter cold, and all their eyes were signed
    with the depths of misery that gnawed inside.   39
I looked about, and then glanced down to find
    two who were pressed together so intimately
    that the hair upon their heads was intertwined.   42
"Tell me," I said to them, "who you may be,
    frozen chest to chest." They craned their necks, and when
    they turned their faces up to look at me,   45
their eyes, which had been only moist within,
    now overflowed. Tears trickled down and froze,
    and locked them even tighter than they'd been.   48
Two boards were never clamped as close as those
    two souls. Like goats they butted head to head
    because such anger held them in its throes.   51
Face down nearby was another of the dead,
    whose ears had broken off in the bitter air.
    "Why reflect yourself in us so long?" he said.   54

"If you really want to know about that pair,
  the valley of the Bisenzio was their father's,°
  who was called Alberto. Then it was theirs to share. 57
They came from the same womb, and there are no others—
  search all Caïna and you'll see it's true—
  more fit to set in aspic than those brothers. 60
Not him whose breast and shadow were run through
  by Arthur, not Focaccia° certainly,
  and not this one whose head blocks off my view, 63
who was Sassol Mascheroni°—which should be,
  if Tuscany is the land from which you came,
  all you have to hear to know his history. 66
So that I need speak no more, know that my name
  was Camiscion de' Pazzi.° I'm waiting till
  Carlino comes to mitigate my blame." 69
Then I saw a thousand faces that the chill
  had purpled, and I shudder to this day
  when I cross a frozen stream, and I always will. 72
And I was shivering as we made our way
  through the endless cold to find that central place
  where all gravity collects. I cannot say 75
whether will or fate or pure chance was the case,
  but, passing among the heads, my foot swung out
  and kicked one hard, directly in the face. 78
He wailed at me and then began to shout:
  "What is this? If you're not here to heap on
  revenge for Montaperti,° why knock me about?" 81
"Master," I said, "let me linger with this one
  so that I may satisfy a mental craving.
  I will walk as fast as need be when I'm done." 84
Then I turned back to the soul, who was still raving,
  while my leader stopped. "Just who are you," I said,
  "to criticize how others are behaving?" 87
"Stomping through Antenora to kick the head
  of anyone that you please, just who are you?"
  he asked. "It would be too much, if you weren't dead." 90

"I'm not dead," I replied, "and if it's true
　　　that you crave fame, it's worth your while to know
　　　that among the others I will name you too."   93
He said: "I crave the opposite. Now go,
　　　get out of here, and leave me to my share,
　　　since you don't know how to flatter souls this low."   96
I answered, as I seized him by the hair
　　　upon his nape: "Now tell me what you're called,
　　　or else you won't have a tuft left anywhere."   99
And he replied: "Go ahead and strip me bald!
　　　I won't tell, or show my face, not if you land
　　　on my head a thousand times and leave it mauled."   102
I took his hair and wrapped it round my hand
　　　as he barked and looked straight down to hide his brow,
　　　and I'd already pulled more than one strand   105
when another shouted: "Bocca, what ails you now?
　　　Your flapping jaws are hard enough to endure.
　　　Now barking? What devil's got you anyhow?"   108
"I don't want to hear another word from your
　　　damned traitor's mouth! To your lasting shame," I cried,
　　　"I will spread the news of you, you can be sure!"   111
"Tell what you want. Just go away," he replied.
　　　"But if you escape this place, take my advice
　　　and speak of him who just stretched his mouth so wide. 114
He took French silver. Now he pays the price.
　　　'I saw the one from Duera,'° you can tell it,
　　　'in the bowl where they keep the sinners packed in ice.' 117
And if they ask what others help to fill it,
　　　right by your side's a Beccheria,° the one
　　　the Florentines paid back with a slit gullet.   120
Gianni de' Soldanieri and Ganelon°
　　　are further along. Tebaldello° is another.
　　　He opened up Faenza before the dawn."   123
After we left him, I saw two together
　　　frozen so close in one hole that the head
　　　of the one was like a hood upon the other.   126

I stood and watched the higher one imbed
 his teeth in the other's nape and brain, and eat
 the way a starving man devours bread.   129
Not even Tydeus° in his savage heat
 gnawed Menalippus's head more passionately
 than this one did to the skull and the soft meat. 132
"O you who show such wild hostility,
 attacking him with bestial violence,
 tell me why," I said, "and if it seems to me 135
that you are justified by his offense
 to take such vengeance, then before I die
 in the world above you shall have recompense, 138
unless my tongue should wither and turn dry."

Canto XXXIII

Ugolino; Archbishop Ruggieri; Fra Alberigo;
The Third Ring: Ptolomea (Traitors to Guests)

He paused in his savage meal and raised his head
    from the one he was destroying in his fit,
    and wiped his mouth upon its hair, and said: 3
"What you ask revives a grief so desperate
    that its recollection tears my heart, even though
    I have yet to tell one single word of it.   6
But if my words are a seed from which will grow
    the fruit of this vile traitor's evil fame,
    then I shall speak, and weep while doing so.   9
I do not know who you are, or how you came
    among us, but from your speech you seem to be
    a Florentine. I should tell you that my name   12
was Count Ugolino,° and this one next to me
    is Archbishop Ruggieri. Now I shall explain
    why I am such a neighbor as you see.   15
How I was seized, and executed then,
    having trusted him while he betrayed and lied—
    there is no need to tell that tale again.   18
But of what you cannot know—the way I died,
    the cruelty of it—hear what I have to say.

Whether he wronged me, you may then decide.   21
A narrow opening in the Mew that they
    call Hunger now in memory of my plight,°
    where prisoners are still to be shut away,   24
had shown me more than once the new moon's light
    when the bad dream came to me that tore in two
    the veil that hides the future from our sight.   27
This man was there, as the lord and master who
    pursued the wolf and his young cubs as they sped
    on the mountain that blocks Lucca from the view°   30
of the Pisans. Trained hounds, lean and eager, led
    while Gualandi, Sismondi, and that other one,
    Lanfranchi,° had been set to run on ahead.   33
The wolves were weary after a short run,
    and then I saw the dogs as their sharp fangs ripped
    into the flesh of the father and every son.   36
It was not yet dawn, but I no longer slept.
    My sons were there with me. Though still asleep,
    they called to me to give them bread, and wept.   39
You are cruel indeed if you can know the deep
    dread that I felt, and not yet shed a tear.
    If not this, what could ever make you weep?   42
The time of our morning meal was drawing near.
    My children were awake. Their dreams had stirred
    in each of them uneasiness and fear.   45
From the base of the horrible tower I now heard
    the door being nailed shut, and I looked into
    the faces of my sons, without a word.   48
I did not weep. I was turned to stone all through.
    They wept. And Anselmuccio spoke up when
    he saw my face, saying: 'Father, what's troubling you?'   51
I shed no tears and I gave no answer then,
    and all that day and night I sat like stone,
    until the sun lit up the world again.   54
As soon as a small ray of sunlight shone
    in the miserable prison, and I could see

from their four faces the aspect of my own,   57
I bit my hands in grief and agony.
    And they, assuming that I acted thus
    for hunger, quickly rose and said to me: 60
'Eat of us, Father. It will hurt us less.
    From you we have this wretched flesh we wear.
    Now it is yours to take away from us.'   63
I calmed myself, to stay them from despair.
    Alas, hard earth, you should have opened wide!
    Two more days passed while we sat silent there.   66
And when it was the fourth day, Gaddo cried:
    'Father, why don't you help me!' I watched him fall
    outstretched before my feet. And there he died.   69
Just as you see me now, I saw them all,
    between the fifth and sixth days, one by one,
    drop down and die. Now blindness cast its pall,   72
and for two more days I crawled from son to son,
    calling to them, who were already dead.
    Then fasting did what misery had not done."   75
With eyes asquint, having finished what he'd said,
    as a dog attacks a bone he turned back to
    his gnawing of the other's wretched head.   78
Pisa, disgrace of all the peoples who
    fill the fair land where *sì* is heard, who show
    no readiness to rise and punish you,   81
let Capraia and Gorgona° shift, and go
    to dam the Arno's mouth so that it may
    drown all your citizens with its overflow!   84
Even if Count Ugolino did betray
    your castles as was reputed, you did wrong
    to put his sons upon the cross that way.   87
New Thebes,° there is no guilt in those so young
    as Uguiccione or Brigata or
    the two already mentioned in my song.   90
We came to another place, where we found more
    who were covered with coarse frost in the bitter chill,

  · but these faced up, unlike the ones before.   93
Here tears themselves make tears impossible.
     The grief is blocked, turning inward when it tries
     to express itself, making pain more painful still,   96
for knots are formed by the first tears each soul cries,
     resembling a crystal visor as they spread
     to fill the hollows that surround the eyes.   99
Although, as with a callus that is dead
     to all sensation, the cold was so severe
     that all the feeling in my face had fled,   102
I thought I felt a wind come blowing clear.
     "Master," I turned to ask, "what forces drive
     this current? Aren't all vapors dead down here?"   105
He answered: "Very soon you will arrive
     where your own eyes will give you your reply,
     with what rains down to keep this breath alive."   108
One wretch inside the cold crust gave a cry:
     "O you two souls, so cruel that you have been
     assigned to go where the very basest lie,   111
pry the hard veils from my face, so that I can
     vent my heart-soaking pain for a bit before
     my tears begin to turn to ice again."   114
"Tell me who you are," I answered, "who implore.
     If I fail to help you then, may I be made
     to go to the bottom of the icy floor."   117
"I am Fra Alberigo,° and I displayed
     the fruits of the evil orchard," he replied.
     "Now, for my figs, with dates I am repaid."   120
And I to him: "Oh, you've already died?"
     "I have no information here," he said,
     "how my body fares up there, on the other side.   123
It often happens that a soul is sped—
     such is Ptolomea's° privilege—to this place
     while Atropos has yet to cut its thread.°   126
So that you may scrape the glazed tears from my face
     more readily, let me also say to you

that as soon as the soul betrays, as in my case,   129
its body is taken by a devil who
    will be master over it in everything
    until its allotted time on earth is through.   132
To this cistern then the soul comes plummeting.
    Still walking the earth, perhaps, is the body of
    this one who is here behind me wintering,   135
as you must know if you just came from above.
    He is Ser Branca d'Oria,° and I'll attest
    that he has been here many years." "Enough,"   138
I said to him, "I believe you are in jest.
    I know that Branca d'Oria is not dead.
    He eats and drinks, he sleeps, and he gets dressed."   141
"Above, in the ditch of the Evilclaws," he said,
    "where the sea of sticky pitch is boiling hot,
    Michel Zanche was not yet deposited   144
when this one, dropping down here like a shot,
    left a devil to fill his body in his place,
    as did his kinsman who was in the plot.   147
So, now reach out your arm and clear my face
    of the ice around my eyes." But I refused.
    Betrayal was true courtesy in this case.   150
Genoans, strangers to the customs used
    by all good men, and filled with every vice,
    how are you still here on the earth you have abused?   153
For, with Romagna's worst, there in the ice
    was one of you, who for his crimes was hurled
    to Cocytus, where even now he pays the price   156
while his body goes on walking in the world.

Canto XXXIV

The Fourth Ring: Judecca (Traitors to Lords and Benefactors);
Satan; Brutus, Cassius, and Judas; Climb from the Bottom of Hell,
Past the Earth's Center, to the Southern Hemisphere

"*Vexilla regis prodeunt inferni*°
    toward where we are," I heard my master say.
    "Look forward now and see if you discern him."   3
When our hemisphere grows dark at close of day
    or when a thick fog breathes, there still may be
    a turning windmill seen from far away.   6
Just such a structure I now seemed to see.
    Then I walked behind my leader. The wind was raw
    and there was nothing else to shelter me.   9
I tremble to make verse of what I saw.
    The souls were covered over in this place
    in ice like glass-embedded bits of straw.   12
Some are lying flat, some standing in their space,
    some with heads and some with soles in the ascent,
    one like a bow with feet bent toward his face.   15
We continued moving forward. On we went
    till we reached a place at which it pleased my guide
    to show me the creature once so radiant.   18

He moved from before me, bade me stop, and cried:
   "Behold Dis! Here behold the place where you
   must summon courage and be fortified."   21
I cannot, reader—do not ask me to—
   describe the way I felt, for I know that I
   lack words to tell how cold and weak I grew.   24
I did not live and yet I did not die,
   deprived of both states. You may realize
   what I then became, if you have the wit to try.   27
From midbreast he stood out above the ice,
   the emperor of that realm of misery.
   And I compare more favorably in size   30
with the giants than would any giant be,
   compared with just his arm. With such a limb,
   how monstrous must be his entirety.   33
If he was fair as he is foul and grim,
   and dared defy his maker, it is well said
   that all suffering and sorrow flow from him.   36
I stared to see three faces on his head,
   one of the greatest wonders I had seen yet.
   The middle one faced forward and was red.   39
The other two were joined to it and set
   above each shoulder's midpoint, and they went
   up to his crown, where all three faces met.   42
The right one had a whitish yellow tint.
   The left one had the appearance of the race
   that comes from where the Nile starts its descent. 45
Two enormous wings spread out below each face,°
   well scaled to such a bird. Never did I see
   such sails on any ship in any place.   48
His wings were featherless and leathery
   just like the long wings of a bat, and since
   he flapped the six of them incessantly,   51
all Cocytus was congealed by three cold winds.
   Tears from his six eyes, mixing with a flow
   of bloody slobber, dripped down his three chins. 54

Just as a hackle mangles flax, a row
    of teeth in each mouth gripped a soul. He made
    three spirits suffer unremitting woe.   57
The one in the front mouth was far less afraid
    of his biting than the raking of his nails.
    At times the spirit's back was wholly flayed.   60
My master said: "That one whose fate entails
    the greatest pain is Judas Iscariot.
    His head is in the mouth, while his body flails.   63
Of the other two, whose heads are hanging out,
    that is Brutus in the black face, whose control
    keeps his tongue silent as he writhes about,   66
and Cassius is that other, sinewy soul.
    Now the night is rising once again, and we
    must take our leave, for we have seen the whole."   69
I clasped his neck, as he commanded me.
    Then he, when the monstrous wings were opened wide,
    making use of place and time efficiently,   72
took hold of the shaggy fur on the devil's side
    and climbed down clump by clump, conveying us
    between the frozen crust and the matted hide.   75
The moment we came to where the thigh joint was,
    the point at which the haunches spread, was when
    my leader with movements pained and strenuous   78
brought his head round to Satan's shanks and then,
    just like a climber, grappled on the hair.
    I thought we had turned back toward hell again.   81
He spoke like a weary man who gasps for air:
    "Hold tight. We need such stairs to leave this place
    where there is so much evil everywhere."   84
And after that, he came out through the space
    in a rock, upon whose edge he seated me.
    Then he moved toward me with a cautious pace.   87
I raised my eyes, expecting I would see
    Lucifer just as he had last appeared,
    but his legs were tapering upward endlessly.   90

How perplexed I was by this I will let the herd
    of dullards judge for themselves, who do not know
    what point I'd passed and what had just occurred.   93
"The sun returns now to mid-tierce,° and so
    you must now stand up again," my master said.
    "The road is hard and we have far to go."   96
It was no palace hall that lay ahead,
    but a natural cellar with a rugged floor
    and little light to show us where it led.   99
"Master," I said when I arose, "before
    I uproot myself from the abyss, I pray
    that you help me understand a little more.   102
Where is the ice? And why is he set this way,
    turned upside down? And how did the sun spin
    so short a transit from the night to day?"   105
And he: "You think we are still where we have been,
    on the other side, where I took hold of the hair
    of the evil worm who gnaws the world from within.   108
As long as I climbed down, you were still there.
    When I turned myself, you were where the halves divide,
    at the center that draws all weights from everywhere.   111
You are under the hemisphere on the opposite side
    from the one that canopies the vast dry land,
    beneath whose zenith he was crucified   114
who was born and lived his life without the brand
    or taint of sinfulness. This little sphere
    is Judecca's other face, where your feet now stand.   117
It is evening there when it is morning here,
    and he whose hair we made a ladder of
    is still secured where you saw him appear.   120
He fell upon this side from the heavens above,
    and the land, in terror as he plummeted,
    used the ocean for a cover as it strove   123
toward our hemisphere. And what was here may have fled,
    rushing upward° as he hurtled through the sky
    and leaving this great cavern in its stead."   126

As far from Beelzebub° as it could lie
    within his tomb is a space that no one knows
    by sight, whose presence is detected by   129
the sound of a trickling rivulet that flows
    through a hollow in the rock that it has lined,
    gently wandering and sloping as it goes.   132
We entered on that hidden road to find
    our way once more into the world of light.
    My leader walked ahead and I behind,   135
without a pause to rest, till we were in sight
    of a hole that showed some few particulars
    of those heavenly things that beautify the night.   138
From there we came outside and saw the stars.°

Notes

CANTO I

1 *Midway through the journey of our life*: The poem is set in 1300, when Dante was thirty-five, halfway through his biblically allotted threescore years and ten.

18 *wherever we may rove*: The planet is the sun, which in Ptolemaic, pre-Copernican cosmology was believed to revolve around the earth, the fixed center of the universe.

30 *lower than the other*: This line is commonly given an allegorical as well as a physical interpretation. The feet are understood to be the limbs of the soul. The fixed foot is the left, representing will, which lags behind the right one, intellect. The fullest discussion of the line is John Freccero's "The Firm Foot on a Journey Without a Guide," in his *Dante: The Poetics of Conversion* (Harvard, 1986).

37 *the break of day*: It is the morning of Good Friday. The sun is in Aries, as it was believed to have been at the time of creation.

60 *on the low ground*: The encounter with the three beasts is one of the most frequently and variously interpreted passages of the poem. Traditionally, the leopard, the lion, and the she-wolf have been understood to represent lust, pride, and avarice, respectively—or, in some interpretations, envy, pride (or arrogance), and avarice (or greed), the qualities ascribed to the Florentines by Ciacco in Canto VI (line 75) and Brunetto Latini in Canto XV (line 67). They have also been associated with incontinence, violence, and fraud, the three categories of sin described by Virgil in Canto XI. Some feel that the leopard must represent fraud, given Dante's reference to the belt, or cord, with which he had hoped to snare that beast (Canto XVI, lines 106–8); there Geryon, who also has a spotted hide, is clearly linked to fraud. If this view is accepted, then the she-wolf represents lust or, more broadly, incontinence. Thus, the she-wolf gives Dante the most trouble because while incontinence is the least grievous category of sin, it is the one to which he is most susceptible.

70 *at the latter end*: Virgil (Publius Vergilius Maro, 70–19 B.C.E.) was born before the reign of Julius Caesar. He was in his mid-twenties when Caesar was assassinated.

75 *after the burning of proud Ilium*: The Trojan prince Aeneas, son of Anchises and the goddess Venus, sailed to Italy after the fall of Troy (Ilium) and became the legendary founder of Rome.

105 *between felt and felt*: This is one of the most obscure and hotly debated passages in the poem. The greyhound has been identified with various historical and religious figures, and has even been taken to signify the second coming of Christ. The most frequently proposed candidate is Can Grande della Scalla, who ruled Verona from 1308 to 1329; his name suggests "great dog," and his native city, Verona, lies between the towns of Feltre and Montefeltro. The "felt" reference has also been interpreted astrologically (the Gemini, Castor and Pollux, were commonly depicted as wearing felt caps), spiritually (an allusion to the Franciscan and Dominican orders), and sociologically (suggestive of humble birth).

108 *gave their life's blood*: Nisus and Euralyus were young Trojan soldiers. Turnus, king of the Rutulians, and Camilla, daughter of the king of the Volscians, were leaders of the indigenous Italian peoples who resisted the Trojan invasion. Enemies in life, they are joined here as patriots and as participants in the events that would lead to the founding of Rome.

122 *with a worthier soul than I*: The worthier soul is Beatrice, whose name signifies "one who makes blessed." Associated with Dante's neighbor Beatrice Portinari (1266–1290), she appears as a living person in his *Vita nuova*, where she is celebrated for both her beauty and her spiritual example.

126 *where his city stands*: As one who lived before Christ, Virgil did not accept Christ as his savior and consequently cannot enter heaven (see Canto IV, lines 31–42). This change of guides midway through the journey suggests that salvation can be achieved only through divine grace, not by reason and virtue alone.

133 *Saint Peter's gate*: Like other details in this canto, Saint Peter's gate has inspired controversy, some maintaining that it alludes to the traditional gate of heaven, which does not appear in the *Divine Comedy*, others that it refers to the gate of purgatory, which does.

CANTO II

9 *your true integrity*: The invocation of the muse, a traditional component of epic poetry. Canto I may be regarded as a proem to the entire *Comedy,* leaving thirty-three cantos for the journey through hell. Both the *Purgatorio* and the

Paradiso, which also begin with such invocations, contain thirty-three cantos, making the complete work exactly one hundred cantos long.

13 *Of Silvius's father*: In the *Aeneid*, Silvius is the son of Aeneas and his second wife, Lavinia, daughter of King Latinus of Latium. In Book VI, Aeneas makes the epic hero's ritual journey to the underworld, where his father's shade reveals to him the coming glories of Rome.

30 *the path to our salvation*: The Chosen Vessel, so described in Acts 9.15, is Saint Paul. In 2 Corinthians 12.1–7, Paul speaks of having been raised to the "third heaven" and alludes to its secret messages. In the *Visio Sancti Pauli*, an early medieval text, there is a description of his journey to hell.

78 *the least-circling heaven's zone*: In Ptolemaic cosmology, the "heaven," or planet, with the "least-circling zone," or smallest orbit, is the moon. Within that zone—the center of the physical universe—is the earth.

94 *In heaven a noble lady*: The Virgin Mary. Her name, like that of Jesus Christ, is never spoken aloud in hell.

97 *She summoned Lucia*: Saint Lucy of Syracuse, a third-century virgin martyr, patroness of those with vision problems, and a symbol of illuminating grace.

102–103 *sitting with the venerable / Rachel*: In Genesis, the wife of Jacob. She is usually taken to be a symbol of the contemplative life and is mentioned again in Canto IV, line 60.

CANTO III

32 *as the horror swirled around my head*: This is a disputed passage in the original: some editions print *error*, others—the majority—prefer *orror*. Those who accept the latter reading often cite the *Aeneid*, Book II, line 559: "At me tum primum saevus circumstetit horror" ("For the first time a savage horror surrounded me").

36 *the lives they'd led*: These souls chose neither good nor evil, the lukewarm scorned by Christ. Rudyard Kipling treats this theme delightfully in his poem "Tomlinson."

60 *the great refusal*: This passage has been taken to refer to Esau, to Pontius Pilate, and to several others. One of the earliest identifications, and certainly the most common, is with Celestine V, whose abdication of the papacy in 1294 led to the ascension of the corrupt Boniface VIII (Boniface, who was still pope in 1300, when the *Inferno* is set, is the object of Dante's scorn at several places in the poem; see note to Canto XIX, line 57). Opposition to this assumption is founded in part on Celestine's canonization in 1313, while Dante was still alive.

94 *My leader told him, "Charon"*: Among the rivers of the underworld, Charon is traditionally represented as the ferryman of the Styx, not the Acheron. He appears in Aristophanes' *Clouds* and in Book VI of the *Aeneid*, where Virgil's physical description of him furnishes Dante with several details.

CANTO IV

60 *he did much laboring*: Israel, meaning "soldier of God," was a name given to Jacob after he wrestled with the angel. His father was Isaac, son of Abraham. Rachel was Jacob's wife. His twelve sons were the founders of the twelve tribes of Israel.

63 *the earliest ones*: Lines 52–63 refer to the legendary harrowing of hell. The "mighty one" of line 53 is Christ. Salvation was impossible until he had redeemed by his crucifixion the taint of original sin. At his death, which occurred roughly fifty years after Virgil's, Christ descended to the underworld to effect the salvation of many worthies who had believed in the prophecies of his coming.

88 *of all bards is he*: Virgil's description of Homer as "the sovereign of all bards" acknowledges the *Aeneid*'s heavy borrowings from the *Iliad* and the *Odyssey* (Dante, who did not read Greek, knew Homer only indirectly).

89 *the second one*: Horace (Quintus Horatius Flaccus, 65–8 B.C.E.), who was known in the Middle Ages more for his satires than for his odes, describes himself as a satirist in the *Ars poetica*.

90 *and Lucan finally*: Lucan (Marcus Annaeus Lucanus, 39–65 C.E.) is the author of *Pharsalia*, an epic concerning the conflict between Caesar and Pompey. The *Metamorphoses* of Ovid (Publius Ovidius Naso, 43 B.C.E.–c. 17 C.E.) provided Dante with his chief source for classical myth.

102 *sixth in their wisdom's congregation*: This apparent nomination of himself as one of the six greatest poets of all time seems at first to be an act of breathtaking hubris on Dante's part. But Dante would have regarded his poetic talent as a God-given attribute, not a personal attainment worthy of boast, and in a poem describing the horrific fates of those who misused their God-given gifts, he can legitimately claim to be employing his, like the poets named here, for the highest ends—a claim that Milton would more overtly make for his own intentions at the beginning of *Paradise Lost* (see also Canto XXVI, lines 19–24).

122 *Aeneas and Hector*: The Electra named here is not the daughter of Agamemnon and Clytemnestra about whom Sophocles and Euripides wrote tragedies, but the daughter of Atlas and mother of Dardanus, the founder of Troy. Aeneas and Hector, leader of the Trojan forces in the *Iliad,* are her descendants.

124 *I saw Camilla and Penthesilea*: Penthesilea, the queen of the Amazons, fought for Troy and was killed by Achilles. For Camilla, see note to Canto I, line 108.

126 *with his daughter Lavinia*: For Latinus and Lavinia, see note to Canto II, line 13.

129 *Alone, apart, was Saladin*: Became sultan of Egypt in 1174 and won some victories against the Crusaders before his defeat by Richard Coeur de Lion. Despite his resistance to the Christian invaders of the Holy Land, Saladin was highly regarded in medieval Europe for his piety, justice, and nobility of spirit. Tarquin was the last of the legendary Roman kings; the rape of Lucretia by his son led to his expulsion by Lucius Junius Brutus, brother of Lucretia and nephew of Tarquin, and thus the establishment of the Republic. Brutus is not to be confused with Caesar's assassin, Marcus Junius Brutus. Julia was the daughter of Caesar and wife of Pompey. Cornelia was the daughter of Scipio Africanus and mother of the Gracchi, the tribunes Caius and Tiberius. Marcia was the wife of Cato the Younger.

138–139 *the world to chance, Empedocles, / Dioscorides*: Pedanius Dioscorides, a first-century Greek physician and author of *De materia medica,* catalogued the properties of plants. Empedocles: Aristotle was translated into Latin in the twelfth and thirteenth centuries and was quickly established as the principal classical philosopher, in large part through Thomas Aquinas's incorporation of his work into a Christian context. The others named here were predecessors or contemporaries of Socrates and Plato; they are all presented as stages along the way to the culmination of thought in "the master of all those who know" (line 131).

140 *Hippocrates, Galen*: Hippocrates (fifth century B.C.E.) and Galen (second century C.E.) were Greek physicians.

141 *Seneca, Cicero, Linus, and Orpheus*: The mythical Greek poets Linus and Orpheus are grouped with the Roman moralists Cicero (Marcus Tullius Cicero, 106–43 B.C.E.) and Seneca (Lucius Annaeus Seneca, 4 B.C.E.–65 C.E.), suggesting an association of poetry with wisdom and moral values.

142 *Ptolemy, Euclid the geometer*: Euclid (third century B.C.E.) wrote the *Elements* of geometry. Ptolemy (Claudius Ptolemaeus, c. 90–168) was the Egyptian astronomer whose *Almagest* outlines his system.

143 *Avicenna, and Averroës*: Ibn Rushd Averroës (1126–1198), Spanish Islamic philosopher, wrote the most important medieval commentary on Aristotle. The Arabic philosopher Avicenna (ibn Sina, 980–1037) was the author of a standard medical textbook. Their inclusion, with that of Saladin, might be seen as a partial mitigation of Dante's hostility to Islam as a schism, as shown by the mosques of the city of Dis (Canto VIII, lines 70–72) and the damnation of Mohammed (Canto XXVIII, line 22ff.).

CANTO V

4 *There Minos*: The son of Zeus and Europa, was king of Crete. Virgil describes him and his brother Rhadamanthus as judges of souls in the underworld (*Aeneid,* Book VI).

34 *before the ruin*: For the explanation of the "ruin" so casually mentioned here, see Canto XII, lines 32–45.

60 *where the sultan reigns today*: Semiramis, legendary queen of Assyria, was reputed to have legalized incest to exculpate her sexual relationship with her son.

62 *betrayed Sichaeus's ashes*: Dido, widow of King Sichaeus of Tyre, was queen of Tyre and then of Carthage. By her affair with Aeneas, she broke her vow to remain faithful to her husband's memory; his abandonment of her led to her suicide. The story of Dido and Aeneas is told in Book IV of the *Aeneid,* the best-known and most celebrated part of the epic.

63 *whom wanton passions drove*: Cleopatra, queen of Egypt, was the mistress of Julius Caesar and of Mark Antony.

66 *to battle love*: Helen was the wife of Menelaus, king of Sparta; her abduction by Paris, son of King Priam of Troy, caused the Trojan War. According to a medieval legend not found in Homer, Achilles fell in love with Priam's daughter Polyxena and, in hope of an assignation with her, was lured into a fatal ambush by Paris.

66-67 *and behold / Tristan*: The lover of Iseult, who was the wife of his uncle, King Mark of Cornwall. Their tragic affair is told in a number of medieval romances.

97 *where I was born*: Ravenna, the city where Dante died in exile and is buried, was the birthplace of Francesca da Rimini, whom Dante calls by name at line 117. Around 1275, a marriage was arranged between her and the physically deformed Gianciotto Malatesta; according to Boccaccio, she was tricked into believing that his handsome younger brother Paolo was her prospective husband. Sometime between 1283 and 1286, Gianciotto found his wife and brother in an adulterous liaison and killed them both. Omitted in Francesca's highly self-serving account are the facts that Paolo was also married and that both he and Francesca had children.

107 *Caïna waits to claim our murderer*: Caïna, described in Canto XXXII, is the first round of Cocytus, the ninth and last circle of hell; named for Cain, it punishes sinners who betrayed family. Caïna "waits" for Gianciotto because his death did not occur until 1304.

127-128 *overthrown / by love*: In the Old French romance *Lancelot du Lac*, Lancelot, one of the knights of the Round Table, fell in love with Guinevere, wife of King Arthur. He lost his purity through their ensuing affair and thus became incapable of discovering the Holy Grail.

137 *The book was a Gallehault*: Because Gallehault, Lancelot's friend and fellow knight, acted as go-between for Lancelot and Guinevere, his name had come to signify "panderer."

CANTO VI

13 *The weird and savage Cerberus*: In classical mythology, Cerberus, the fierce three-headed dog, guards the entrance to Hades. In Book VI of the *Aeneid*, the Sybil distracts him with honeyed cake, allowing the living Aeneas to elude his vigilance. The mixture of human attributes with canine ones is Dante's invention.

52-53 *you citizens bestowed / on me*: Attempts have been made to identify this character with a poet called Ciacco dell'Anguillaia, but there is nothing to support the connection beyond the coincidence of names. The text suggests that Ciacco was a nickname, one he did not especially enjoy. Since *ciacco* connotes "pig" or "hog," it is tempting to assume that he was so called because of his gluttony, but it is not clear whether the word had this meaning before Dante's use of it.

75 *envy, arrogance, and greed*: This is the first of the prophecies made by condemned souls at various points in the poem. Ciacco predicts events that were still in the future in April 1300, but that occurred, of course, before the writing of the *Inferno*. After driving the Ghibellines out of Florence in 1289, the Guelph party had split into rival factions, the White ("the rustic sect," to which Dante belonged, so called because its leaders, the Cerchi family, were from outside the city) and the Black ("the other one"); their rivalry flared into open warfare on May 1, 1300, and the Blacks were expelled the following year. The temporizer of line 69 is almost certainly the reviled Pope Boniface VIII, whose support of the Blacks enabled them to retake the city in 1302, sending the Whites into exile—an exile which for Dante would prove permanent. The identities of the two just men, who are in any event insufficient for the city's salvation, have not been positively established.

87 *you will see them there*: As Ciacco suggests he will, Dante subsequently encounters Farinata degli Uberti (Canto X, line 32), Tegghiaio Aldobrandi and Jacopo Rusticucci (Canto XVI, lines 40–45), and Mosca dei Lamberti (Canto XXVIII, line 106). Oddly, Arrigo, who has never been positively identified, makes no appearance in the *Inferno* and is not mentioned again.

106 *What does your science say?*: The science in question is the philosophy of Aristotle, in his *De anima,* and the commentary on it by Thomas Aquinas in the *Summa theologica.*

115 *the great enemy*: The reference is either to Pluto, the god of the underworld (also known as Hades), or to Plutus, the god of wealth—or possibly to both, since even in classical times they were often thought of in terms of one another. Obviously, in Dantean terms either one would qualify as a "great enemy" of humanity.

CANTO VII

1 Pape Satàn, pape Satàn aleppe!: Discussion of the meaning of this line has been extensive and wide-ranging. Some claim that it is mere gibberish, but that interpretation seems implausible: the third line suggests that Virgil understands what Plutus is saying, and the terms Plutus uses do resemble recognizable words. The most common interpretation is that Plutus is invoking Satan as father or pope. With *aleppe*, which suggests the Hebrew *aleph*, he might be either claiming the primacy of Satan or crying out a variation on *alas.*

12 *avenged the arrogant offense*: Lucifer's rebellion against God led to the expulsion of the rebel angels from heaven by the archangel Michael.

22 *that swirl above Charybdis*: In Book XII of the *Odyssey,* Odysseus must navigate around the whirlpool Charybdis, located in the Strait of Messina. Dante would have been more familiar with Charybdis through references in Ovid, Lucan, and the *Aeneid.*

38 *on our left side*: The placement of the avaricious on the left side suggests that their sin is worse than that of their opposites, the spendthrifts.

99 *have now begun to sink*: Virgil's words indicate that it is now past midnight.

CANTO VIII

3 *gleaming at its very top*: From Boccaccio in the fourteenth century to Giorgio Padoan (*Il lungo cammino del "Poema sacro": Studi danteschi,* Florence) in 1993, the opening of this canto has led commentators to speculate that some time elapsed between the writing of the first seven cantos and a resumption at this point; such arguments have not drawn much support. Dante does, however, pursue an unusual narrative strategy here, an extended flashback until line 80, when Virgil and Dante arrive at the tower mentioned in the last line of Canto VII.

19 *Phlegyas, Phlegyas*: Here, the boatman of the river Styx. In classical mythology, he was the son of the war god Ares and a human mother, and was the father of Coronis, who was seduced by Apollo. To avenge his daughter, Phlegyas burned the temple of Apollo at Delphi, for which the god killed him and condemned him to punishment in the underworld. As a shade, he appears briefly in Book VI of the *Aeneid,* warning others against such rashness toward the gods. John Ciardi notes: "Dante's choice of a ferryman is especially apt. Phlegyas is the link between the Wrathful (to whom his paternity relates him) and the Rebellious Angels who menaced God (as he menaced Apollo)" (*The Inferno,* Rutgers, 1954).

61 *Let's get Filippo Argenti*: Filippo de Cavicciuoli was a member of the Adimari family, who were of the Black faction of the Guelphs (see note to Canto VI, line 75). Of great wealth and short temper, he was supposedly called "Argenti" because he had his horse shod with silver. According to early accounts, his brother came into possession of some of Dante's property after the poet's exile from Florence.

69 *a somber population*: Dis was another name for Pluto, the Roman god of the underworld, equivalent to the Greek Hades, and by further equivalence another name for Lucifer or Satan. The "huge brigade" are the angels who followed Lucifer in his rebellion against God and were "cast out / and rained from heaven" (lines 82–83).

71 *all its mosques aglow*: The mosques suggest the medieval Christian view of Islam as a heresy, a rebellion against God. Also, as Bernard Lewis says of medieval and Renaissance references to Islam: "In poetry and polemic, in history and literature, they reflect the consciousness of a Christian Europe besieged and threatened by a mighty and expanding Islamic world, a Europe that in a sense was defined and delimited by the frontiers of Muslim power in the east, the southeast, and the south" (*Cultures in Conflict,* Oxford, 1995).

96 *I would never come back here*: The earth, where Dante is writing his account.

125 *at a less secret gate*: The entrance to hell described at the beginning of Canto III. Christ forced open the outer portal in his harrowing of hell (see note to Canto IV, line 63), despite the opposition of Satan and his followers.

CANTO IX

23 *conjured by cruel Erichtho*: In Book VI of Lucan's *Pharsalia,* Erichtho, a sorceress of Thessaly, reanimates a dead soldier of Pompey's army at the behest of the general's son, Sextus, who wishes to learn in advance the outcome of the campaign against Caesar (48 B.C.E.). There is no known source for the incident that Virgil describes in lines 22–27, and it is generally assumed to be of Dante's invention.

27 *where Judas is confined*: Judecca is the fourth and last region of the ninth and last circle of hell (see Canto XXXIV).

48 *The one in the center is Tisiphone*: The Furies, also known as Erinyes or Eumenides, appear in many classical works, most notably the *Oresteia* of Aeschylus, as avengers of crimes, especially those that violate the bonds of kinship. They are presented as the gatekeepers of the city of Dis in Book VI of the *Aeneid.*

52 *Now let Medusa*: The Gorgons were three sisters, of whom the beautiful Medusa was the youngest. After her rape by Neptune (Ovid's *Metamorphoses,* Book IV), the goddess Minerva gave her serpents for hair, making her appearance so horrifying that all who saw her were turned to stone.

54 *when Theseus was so bold!*: In the version followed by Dante, Theseus, king of Athens, entered the underworld to carry off Proserpine, wife of Hades, and was imprisoned there until Hercules rescued him.

63 *the hidden doctrine may be found*: Commentators are divided on the meaning of these lines, not only in their interpretations of "the hidden doctrine" but also on whether the "strange lines" are the ones preceding or following this address to the reader.

99 *those who try can anticipate*: When Hercules came to hell to rescue Theseus (see note to line 54), he chained Cerberus and dragged him on the ground.

116 *with some lower and some higher*: These lines refer to ancient Roman cemeteries, with sarcophagi of varying heights, in Provence and in Istria (Croatia).

CANTO X

12 *will all be sealed eternally*: According to Joel 3.2, Jehoshaphat, a valley between Jerusalem and the Mount of Olives, will be the site of the last judgment, when all will reclaim their bodies and return with them to heaven or hell.

13 *in this section Epicurus lies*: The Greek philosopher Epicurus (342–270 B.C.E.) maintained that all events are subject to natural, not supernatural, explanation, and that the greatest good is pleasure (not sensuality, but freedom from pain and anxiety), which is achieved through virtue, temperance, and harmony of mind and body. His philosophy denied divine intervention and punishment and the immortality of the soul.

31–32 *Turn round and view / Farinata*: Manente degli Uberti, called Farinata, was born early in the thirteenth century, and in 1239 became leader of the Ghibellines, who expelled the Guelphs from Florence in 1248. The Guelphs returned three years later and in 1258 expelled the Ghibellines, who drove them out once again in 1260 at the bloody battle of Montaperti, near the river Arbia (see lines 85–86). After the battle, a council was held in Empoli, at which Farinata argued successfully against the intention of the Pisan Ghibellines to destroy Florence (see lines 91–93). Farinata died in 1264, the year before Dante's birth. In 1283, he and his wife, who had disbelieved in the resurrection of Christ, were posthumously branded heretics.

62–63 *it may be, / your Guido*: The shade to whom Dante is speaking is Cavalcante de' Cavalcanti (died c. 1280), a leader of the Guelphs. His son was the poet Guido Cavalcanti (whose works were translated by Dante Gabriel Rossetti and Ezra Pound). In the *Vita nuova*, Dante had earlier described Guido as his "first friend." In an effort to heal political strife, Guido Cavalcanti was married to Farinata's daughter Beatrice. Farinata's later remarks (lines 100–105) explain why Cavalcante is unaware that his son Guido is alive in April 1300 (and that he will die in August of that year), while Farinata can apparently tell the future. Lines 61–63 are ambiguous, no doubt deliberately so. Even the syntax is not entirely clear, since the object of Guido's disdain can be either Virgil or, in the reading I have followed, the one to whom Virgil is conducting Dante—which can mean either Beatrice or God. The heretical views of the Cavalcanti family would seem to support the latter interpretation.

81 *just how much it weighs*: "The lady who reigns here" is Hecate, or Proserpine, wife of Hades; she was commonly identified with the moon. Fifty months or so after this prophecy, in the summer of 1304, the Whites made their last, futile attempt to reenter Florence, after which Dante saw no prospect of the end of his exile.

108 *when the door of time is shut*: After the last judgment, time will no longer exist.

119 *the second Frederick and the Cardinal* . . . : Ottaviano degli Ubaldini (d. 1273), who was suspected of unbelief and is reputed to have said, "If I have a soul, I have lost it a thousand times for the Ghibellines." His nephew Archbishop Ruggieri is among the most deeply damned (see Canto XXXIII and its first note). Frederick II (1194–1250), king of Sicily and Naples, Holy Roman Emperor, was known as *stupor mundi*, "the wonder of the world," for his political skills, his intellectual accomplishments and fostering of learning, and his open mind and humanistic spirit. Although himself a scourge of heretics, he was suspected of Epicureanism by the Guelphs; the latter part of his reign was marked by constant struggles with the papacy, and he was excommunicated.

CANTO XI

9 *from the path of righteousness*: There is a possible confusion here between Pope Anastasius II (496–98) and the emperor Anastasius I (491–518). Photinus, a deacon of Thessalonica, is believed to have persuaded the emperor to the heresy of Acacius, which denied the divinity of Christ. On the other hand, Robert and Jean Hollander point out that Isidore of Seville, a possible source for Dante's lines, says that Pope Anastasius was converted by Photinus, bishop of Sirmium, to the Ebionite heresy, which claimed that Jesus was the purely human child of Mary and Joseph (*Dante Alighieri: Inferno*, Doubleday, 2000).

50 *Sodom and Cahors*: Cahors, a city in southern France, was notorious in the Middle Ages for usury. "Sodom" connotes sodomy.

80 *in the pages of your* Ethics: Aristotle's *Nicomachean Ethics* is cited. For Aristotle, "bestiality," or brutishness, is a category that transcends the normal range of human evil to encompass such things as cannibalism; since the *Inferno* groups violence and fraud under malice, there has been much debate over what Dante intends by the term.

101 *If you read your* Physics: The reference is to the *Physics* of Aristotle, although this discussion of usury more likely derives from the commentary of Aquinas on Aristotle's *Politics*.

108 *and earn their bread*: See Genesis 3.19: "In the sweat of thy face shalt thou eat bread, till thou return unto the ground."

115 *the cliff we must descend*: The Wain is the Big Dipper, and the Fish are the constellation Pisces. It is now about four o'clock in the morning, and ten of the journey's twenty-four hours have elapsed.

CANTO XII

6 *being badly shored*: The precipice of Slavini di Marco, south of Trent in northern Italy, was formed by a landslide around 883, which diverted the river Adige from its course.

13 *the infamy of Crete*: Minos, king of Crete, failed to carry out the promised sacrifice of a bull to the sea god Poseidon, who afflicted Minos's wife, Pasiphaë, with an unnatural passion for a bull. She lured the bull by crouching inside a wooden cow covered with cowhide. From this union was born the Minotaur, which Minos kept imprisoned in an intricate labyrinth. It is usually represented as having a bull's head and a human body.

20 *by your sister's guidance*: Theseus, king of Athens, killed the Minotaur with the assistance of Ariadne, daughter of Minos and Pasiphaë, who provided him with a sword and a long thread by which to find his way back out of the labyrinth.

45 *all came crashing down just then*: In Matthew 27.50–53, the earth is convulsed by a mighty earthquake at the moment of Christ's death upon the cross.

55 *a single file of centaurs race*: The original centaurs, one hundred in number, were passionate and violent creatures, half man, half horse. They were born when Ixion, seeking to possess Hera, instead assaulted a cloud that Zeus had fashioned to resemble her, and the drops of his seed fell to the earth.

64–65 *We will reply instead / to Chiron*: The son of Philyra and of Kronos, the sun god, who had turned himself into a horse to elude his wife's jealousy. Wise and just, Chiron was the tutor of Achilles, Jason, Asclepius, and others.

69 *upon his very slayer*: Nessus, one of the sons of Ixion, carried Deianira, wife of Hercules, across a stream. Attempting to rape her, he was shot by Hercules with a poisoned arrow. Dying, the centaur told her to keep some of his blood, which, he claimed, when smeared on a garment, would cause its wearer to love her. Hercules later fell in love with Iole, Deianira gave him the garment, and its poison caused him such horrible suffering that he committed suicide (Ovid, *Metamorphoses*, Book IX).

71–72 *The other one / is Pholus*: Another of Ixion's sons, died accidentally when he dropped one of Hercules' poisoned arrows on his foot.

107 *cruel Dionysius too*: The likeliest identifications are Alexander of Macedonia, the Great (356–323 B.C.E.), and Dionysus the Elder, who ruled Syracuse from 405 to 367 B.C.E.

109–110 *such black hair grew / is Azzolino*: Ezzelino III da Romano (1194–1259), son-in-law of Frederick II, was a Ghibelline leader who committed atrocities, especially against the Paduans.

110–111 *that fairhaired one / is Opizzo d'Esti*: Obizzo II d'Este (1247–1293), lord of Ferrara and a Guelph, is believed to have been smothered by his son and successor, Azzo VIII. Various attempts have been made to explain "stepson" (line 112): some see it as a hint at the infidelity of Obizzo's wife, others as a suggestion of the unnaturalness of his son's crime.

120 *to this very day*: "That one" is Guy de Montfort (c. 1243–1298), of royal English blood. To avenge his father, Simon de Montfort, killed at the battle of Evesham in 1265 by the future Edward I, Guy stabbed Edward's cousin, Prince Henry of Cornwall, at mass in the church of San Silvestro in Viterbo in 1271. According to one source, Henry's heart was placed in a golden casket on a pillar at the end of London Bridge. It continues to drip because Henry's murder remains unavenged.

133 *Heavenly justice stings Attila*: Attila (c. 406–453), king of the Huns (c. 433–53), was known as the Scourge of God.

135 *Pyrrhus and Sextus*: Both identifications are disputed, but Pyrrhus is probably the king of Epirus (318–272 B.C.E.) whose defeat of the Romans at Asculum in 279 was the original Pyrrhic victory, and Sextus is most likely Sextus Pompeius Magnus (d. 35 B.C.E.), younger son of Pompey the Great.

136 *the two Riniers*: Rinier da Corneto and Rinier Pazzo were highway robbers of Dante's time, the former near Rome and the latter south of Florence.

CANTO XIII

8 *between Corneto and Cécina*: The reference is to the rough terrain of the Maremma in Tuscany, bounded on the north by the river Cecina and on the south by the Marta, on which the town of Corneto is situated.

15 *in the twisted trees*: The Harpies, daughters of Thaumas and Electra, were usually represented as birds with the faces of women and as defilers of food. In Book III of the *Aeneid*, they chase the Trojans from the Strophades islands with prophecies of famine and starvation.

48 *in the pages of my poetry*: In Book III of the *Aeneid*, Aeneas breaks the branch of a myrtle bush, and from it comes the voice of the murdered Polydorus, a son of King Priam, who is buried beneath the plant.

59 *to Frederick's heart*: The speaker is Pier delle Vigne (c. 1190–1249), a trusted counselor and minister of Emperor Frederick II. After a long and successful career, he was accused of treachery, blinded, and thrown into prison, where he committed suicide. His speech in this canto reflects the rhetorically ornate style both of his official documents, written in Latin, and of his vernacular poetry.

64 *who never turns aside her stare*: The reference is to envy.

123 *his breath was nearly gone*: Arcolano Maconi of Siena and Giacomo da Sant'Andrea of Padua were notorious spendthrifts and squanderers of their property. Maconi died in 1288 in a bloody encounter between the Sienese and the Aretines at the crossing of the Pieve del Toppo, reputedly choosing to die in battle rather than to escape and live in poverty.

139 *to see this shameful rout*: The speaker of these lines has not been positively identified. According to legend as reported in the early commentaries, in pagan times the Florentines chose Mars, the god of war, as their patron. When the city was converted to Christianity, Mars was replaced by Saint John the Baptist, but the statue of Mars was preserved in a tower, in order to avoid the god's displeasure. When Florence was destroyed by Attila in 450, the tower—and the statue—fell into the Arno. When the city was rebuilt by Charlemagne early in the ninth century, the statue was recovered and placed on a pillar by the river, where it remained until it was swept away by a flood in 1333.

149 *ashes left by Attila*: Florence was in fact besieged by Totila, king of the Ostrogoths, in 542, not by Attila nearly a century earlier. There is no evidence that the city was destroyed by Totila—or by Attila or by anyone else—and then rebuilt by Charlemagne.

CANTO XIV

15 *Cato marched with his command*: Cato the Younger (95–46 B.C.E.) led his army through the northern Sahara in Libya to escape Caesar's forces after the defeat of Pompey. Dante adapts a reference from Lucan's *Pharsalia,* in which Cato refuses to be carried, as was customary, and instead marches on foot with his soldiers.

31 *And just as Alexander*: Dante here cites the *De meteoris* of Albertus Magnus (c. 1200–1280), who misrecalls an incident in the (probably spurious) *Epistoli Alexandri,* in which Alexander the Great supposedly describes to his tutor, Aristotle, how he had ordered his soldiers to trample the snow.

46 *who is that great one*: Capaneus was one of the seven against Thebes, as recounted in the *Thebaid,* an epic poem by Statius (Publius Papinius Statius, c. 40–96 C.E.). With the aid of an army and seven mighty champions, Polynices, son of Oedipus, besieged the city when his brother Eteocles refused to relinquish power to him as previously agreed. As he scaled the city wall, Capaneus defied Jove, who slew him with a thunderbolt.

56 *of dark Mongibello's*: Mongibello is Mount Etna in Sicily, where Vulcan had his forge.

58 *at the field of Phlegra*: At Phlegra, Jove defeated the giants who were storming Mount Olympus.

79 *Down from the Bulicame*: A hot spring, near Viterbo, where a spa developed. According to Boccaccio, a stream was diverted from the spring to serve the needs of the many local prostitutes, who were not allowed to use the public baths.

95 *a wasteland now, called Crete*: The Mediterranean island of Crete was once believed to be the center of the world. According to the *Aeneid*, it was the source of Trojan—and therefore of Roman—civilization. Its king was Saturn (equivalent to the Greek Kronos).

102 *when the child would cry*: Saturn devoured each of his children to prevent the fulfillment of the prophecy that he would be overthrown by one of them. His wife, Rhea, hid their son Jupiter (or Jove) to spare him this fate.

105 *Damietta in the east*: The statue is derived from the dream of Nebuchadnezzar (Daniel 2.31–35), but its placement within Mount Ida is apparently Dante's invention. According to Charles S. Singleton, the Egyptian city of Damietta may have been identified in the Middle Ages with Memphis, the seat of the Pharaohs (*Dante Alighieri: The Divine Comedy. Inferno 2: Commentary,* Princeton, 1970).

119 *they form Cocytus*: Cocytus is the frozen lake at the pit of hell (Cantos XXXIII–XXXIV).

138 *purged guilt from the soul*: In Latin poetry, Lethe is the river of forgetfulness, whose waters are drunk by souls about to be reincarnated. Dante places it at the summit of the Mount of Purgatory.

CANTO XV

9 *from the Carentana*: Chiarentana is a mountainous region north of Padua. Wissant and Bruges are in Flanders. In both areas, dikes were constructed to prevent flooding.

30 *and answered: "Ser Brunetto"*: Brunetto Latini (c. 1220–1294) was a notary (hence the title *Ser*) and a prominent Guelph. He lived in France from 1260 to 1294, during a Ghibelline ascendancy, and was afterward active in public affairs in Florence. His principal volume was *Li Livres dou Tresor*, an encyclopedic work in French prose. His *Tesoretto* is a long allegorical and didactic poem in Italian, which influenced Dante in the writing of the *Comedy*. There is no other surviving or known source for the identification of Brunetto as a homosexual.

78 *into corruption's nest*: As did Farinata in Canto X, Brunetto prophesies Dante's exile from Florence. These lines draw upon the legend, retold by Brunetto in his *Tresor*, that Florence was founded by the Romans after the siege of nearby Fiesole, where Catiline had fled after the failure of his conspiracy (63 B.C.E.), and that the Fiesolans, including Catiline's followers, intermingled with the Roman settlers.

89 *with another text, which a lady*: Beatrice; "another text": the prophecy of Farinata.

108–109 *by the same offense. / Here Priscian*: A celebrated Latin grammarian of the early sixth century. The little that survives concerning him says nothing about homosexuality.

110 *with Francesco d'Accorso*: Francesco d'Accorso (1225–1293) was born in Bologna, where he became—as his father had been in Florence—a lawyer and a professor of civil law. In 1273, he went to England at the invitation of Edward I, and was for a time a lecturer at Oxford.

114 *the distended nerves he had defiled*: Andrea de' Mozzi was bishop of Florence from 1287 to 1295, when he was transferred to Vicenza on the Bacchiglione because of his scandalous ways. He died in February 1296. Since the pope who transferred him was Boniface VIII, the traditional description of the pontiff as "the servant of servants" has a satirical application here.

124 *who wins the prize*: The race in question, in which the runners competed naked, was established in 1207 and held on the first Sunday in Lent.

CANTO XVI

37 *The good Gualdrada*: The daughter of Bellincione Berti, Gualdrada when young supposedly impressed Emperor Otto IV with her beauty, intelligence, and modesty. Unfortunately for legend, she was married in 1180, twenty years before Otto became emperor and nearly thirty before he visited Florence.

38 *He was Guido Guerra*: A Guelph leader (1220–1272) on the field of battle. He advised the Florentine Guelphs against the planned Sienese campaign of 1260; his counsel was disregarded, with disastrous results.

41 *is Tegghiaio Aldobrandi*: Another leader of the Florentine Guelphs, who also counseled against the Sienese expedition.

44 *was Iacopo Rusticucci*: Jacopo Rusticucci was apparently a middle-class merchant, and thus the social inferior of his two companions. According to early commentators, his wife was so shrewish that he sent her back to her family.

70 *Guiglielmo Borsiere*: Little is known of Guiglielmo Borsiere, whose surname suggests "pursemaker." He is the protagonist of one of the tales in Boccaccio's *Decameron*.

100 *San Benedetto dell'Arpe*: A monastery near the source of the Montone, a river northeast of Florence that runs to the Adriatic.

CANTO XVII

1 *with the pointed tail*: The monster is identified as Geryon at line 97 of the canto. In classical mythology, he was the treacherous three-headed or three-bodied king of an island in the far western stream Oceanus and the possessor of a fabled herd of cattle. He was killed by Hercules as part of his tenth labor, that of the oxen of the sun. He is mentioned in the *Aeneid* and in Ovid's *Heroides*. Dante's depiction of him draws upon his tripartite nature, but incorporates details from the plague of locusts in Revelations and from the manticore as described in Pliny's *Historia naturalis* and in the *Tresor* of Brunetto Latini.

18 *such rich brocade*: Arachne challenged the goddess Athene (Minerva to the Romans) to a weaving competition. Arachne's tapestry depicted the amours of the gods. Angered by its subject, unable to find any flaw in its craftsmanship, Minerva destroyed the design of Arachne, who hanged herself. The goddess, however, saved her and changed her into a spider. Ovid tells the story in Book VI of the *Metamorphoses*.

60 *by its shape and bearing*: The azure lion on a yellow background was the heraldic device of the Gianfigliazzi family of Florence, prominent Black Guelphs and accused usurers.

63 *that was red as blood*: The white goose on the blood-red field denotes the Ubriachi family, Ghibelline bankers and moneychangers.

65 *a gross blue sow*: The white purse with the blue sow signifies the Scrovegni family of Padua. The speaker is usually identified as Reginaldo degli Scrovegni, who became very wealthy through the practice of usury and died around 1290.

68 *my townsman Vitaliano*: This line is customarily understood to refer to Vitaliano del Dente, who was appointed mayor of Padua in 1307, and was described as a moneylender.

72 *the sovereign cavalier*: Assumed to be Giovanni Buiamonte, of the Becchi family of Florence, a moneylender who was made a knight sometime before 1298.

108 *with a scar still visible*: Phaëthon persuaded his father, the sun god Helios, to let him drive the chariot of the sun. He was unable to control the horses, and Zeus slew him with a thunderbolt to keep the earth from catching fire. The scar on the sky is the Milky Way. The story is related in Book II of the *Metamorphoses*.

111 *his feathers fell away*: On a second flight, Icarus ignored the warnings of his father, Daedalus, and flew too near the sun, which melted the wax that held the feathers of his wings, and he fell into the sea and drowned (*Metamorphoses*, Book VIII).

CANTO XVIII

2–3 *that is known / as Malebolge*: A word ("Evilditches") coined by Dante, combining the terms for "evil" (*male*) and "ditch" or "pouch" (*bolgia*).

34 *the castle before them*: In February 1300, Pope Boniface VIII proclaimed that year to be one of Jubilee (the first such in the church's history), during which indulgences would be granted to those who visited the basilicas of Saints Peter and Paul. The heavy traffic on the Ponte Angelo over the Tiber (it is estimated that as many as 200,000 people visited Rome that year) was controlled in the manner described here: one file of pilgrims crossing the bridge with the Castel Sant'Angelo directly in view, on their way to Saint Peter's, and the other file crossing toward Monte Giordano and Saint Paul's.

50 *Venedico Caccianemico*: Venedico Caccianemico (born c. 1228) was for many years a leader of the Bolognese Guelphs. Although Dante apparently believes that he was dead by 1300, documents indicate that he survived until 1302 or early 1303.

57 *she might do his will*: Venedico was rumored to have procured his sister, "the lovely" Ghisola ("Ghisalobella"), for Obizzo II, the marchese d'Este (see note to Canto XII, line 111), either for a bribe or in order to win favor.

60–61 *clear through / to the Reno*: The rivers Sàvena and Reno mark the western and eastern boundaries of the city. *Sipa*: old Bolognese dialect for "yes."

96 *Medea has her vengeance too*: Jason, leader of the Argonauts, was promised the throne of Iolcus if he could return with the golden fleece belonging to King Aeëtes of Colchis. On the way, he stopped at the island of Lemnos, where the women had massacred all the men. Hypsipyle, the daughter of King Thoas, had deceived the other women by hiding her father and pretending to have killed him. Jason won the fleece with the aid of Aeëtes' daughter Medea, whom he brought back with him and married. He later deserted her for Glauce, daughter of King Creon of Corinth. On their wedding day, Medea killed the bride and her own two children by Jason.

117 *who could guess?*: Under ordinary circumstances, a priest's tonsure would distinguish him from a layman.

122 *you are Alessio Interminei*: The Interminei (or Interminelli) family were prominent members of the White party in Lucca. Little is known of Alessio.

133 *Are you greatly pleased with me?*: A flattering courtesan in *Eunuchus*, a comedy by Terence (Publius Terentius Afer, c. 195–159 B.C.E.).

CANTO XIX

1 *O Simon Magus!*: In Acts 8.9–24, Simon the magician was converted to Christianity by the preaching of Philip. When he saw Peter and John summon the holy spirit, he offered them money to acquire this power for himself, and was sternly rebuked. From his name comes the word *simony*, which signifies a trafficking in holy things, especially the buying and selling of ecclesiastical offices.

21 *to open all men's eyes*: There is no documentation of the incident that Dante describes here. Some have argued the unlikelihood of his gratuitously interpolating a self-defense against a charge of sacrilege, and have instead suggested that the last clause has larger thematic and theological implications. For one such interpretation, see Mark Musa, *Dante Alighieri's* Divine Comedy. Inferno: Commentary (Indiana, 1996), pp. 257–59.

50 *a killer who, placed inside*: In the Middle Ages, an assassin would be executed by being placed upside down in a ditch and buried alive.

57 *the lovely lady that you lacerated*: Pope Boniface VIII (Benedetto Caetani, 1235–1303) is the subject of numerous gibes in the course of the poem. The speaker mistakes Dante for Boniface, who is not due to arrive for another three and a half years. The lovely lady that he tore to pieces by his corrupt practices is, of course, the church; "guile" alludes to the common belief that Boniface had persuaded his predecessor, Celestine V (see note to Canto III, line 60), to resign, and then won the support of King Charles II of Naples in his effort to become pope himself.

69 *the great mantle was my own*: The speaker is Giovanni Gaetano degli Orsini (whose surname means "little bears"), Pope Nicholas III (1277–80).

87 *will pay heed*: Nicholas has been dead for nearly twenty years, and must wait another three for his replacement, Boniface, whose own feet will be exposed and aflame for only eleven years until he is pushed along by the arrival of the even more corrupt Clement V in 1314. Clement, born Bertrand de Got in Gascony, intrigued with King Philip IV of France to win the papacy, offering him a share of the church's revenues. Upon his accession, Clement moved the papal see to Avignon (where it remained until 1377) and created nine new French cardinals. In 2 Maccabees 4–5, Jason becomes high priest of the Jews by bribing King Antiochus of Syria and proceeds to introduce corrupt practices. He is soon displaced, however, by Menelaus, who offers the king an even greater bribe.

95 *gold or silver from Matthias*: In Acts 1.13–26, Matthias is selected by lot to take Judas's place among the Apostles.

99 *that you guard them well*: This is probably a reference to the now discredited assumption that Nicholas III was bribed to support Giovanni da Procida, a force behind the bloody uprising known as the Sicilian Vespers (1282), which liberated Sicily from the rule of Charles I of Anjou.

111 *his delight in purity*: In Revelations 17, John gives his vision of pagan Rome, which Dante applies to the corrupt papacy. The seven heads are here understood to be the sacraments, and the ten horns are the commandments, whose power waned when the church's husband, the pope, turned away from virtue.

117 *you as his own*: Constantine I (c. 274–337), known as the Great, was Roman emperor from 306 to 337. Dante alludes to the Donation of Constantine, a document forged in the papal curia and believed genuine for seven hundred years until its fraudulence was demonstrated in the fifteenth century. It claims that, in return for Constantine's being cured of leprosy by Pope Sylvester I (see note to Canto XXVII, line 95), this "first rich father" and all succeeding popes were granted temporal sovereignty over the western part of the empire, including Italy.

CANTO XX

32–33 *raised the call / 'Amphiaraus'*: The seer Amphiaraus was one of the seven against Thebes (see note to Canto XIV, line 46). As he had foreseen, he died in battle during the siege, when the earth opened to swallow him as he was retreating.

39–40 *of his shoulder blades. / See Tiresias*: The Theban Tiresias was turned into a woman when he struck a pair of copulating snakes. After seven years, he struck them again and was returned to his male form. When summoned to settle a dispute between Zeus and Hera over whether males or females enjoyed lovemaking more, he agreed with Zeus, stating that women experienced ten times as much sexual pleasure. For this, Hera struck him blind, and Zeus compensated him with the gift of prophecy. His story is told in Book III of Ovid's *Metamorphoses*. He appears most famously in Sophocles' *Oedipus the King* and T. S. Eliot's *The Waste Land*, as well as in the *Odyssey* (as a shade) and several plays by Euripides.

46–47 *in the chain / is Aruns*: An Etruscan soothsayer who, in Lucan's *Pharsalia*, foresaw but did not fully communicate the consequences of the war between Caesar and Pompey. According to Lucan, he lived in the ruins of Luni and divined by, among other things, examining entrails. It is Dante who situates him in a nearby cave and makes him, by implication, an astrologer.

54–55 *on that side too, / was Manto*: The daughter of Tiresias. In Book X of the *Aeneid,* Manto is described as coming to Italy after her father's death and the fall of Thebes, and giving birth to Ocnus after mating with the river god Tiber.

77–78 *it travels then / to Govèrnolo*: The town of Governolo is some twelve miles from Mantua. Benaco was the Latin name for Lake Garda, at the foot of the Tyrolean Alps. The city of Garda is on its eastern shore. Valcamonica is a valley west of the lake. The term *Pennino* alludes to the Alpine range (although precisely which part of it is alluded to is a matter of some dispute). The boundaries of the dioceses of Brescia, Trent, and Verona meet at a point in the middle of Lake Garda, at the southern end of which stand the fortress and town of Peschiera.

93 *the name the people chose*: By some accounts, it was customary in the ancient world to determine the names of cities through the casting of lots.

96 *the cunning Pinamonte's calculation*: Alberto da Casalodi, a Guelph count from Brescia, was ruler of Mantua in 1272 and much resented by the native population. The Ghibelline Pinamonte Bonacolsi duped him into thinking that he could hold onto power only by exiling the city's noble families, which he did to such an extent that he deprived himself of his own supporters. Pinamonte led a revolt that resulted in the exile of Casalodi and the murders of the remaining nobles.

99 *devalue what is true*: This statement of Virgil's has occasioned much comment, especially since his account here contradicts the one in the *Aeneid* (see note to line 55 above). The matter is further complicated by the mention of "the daughter of Tiresias" as one of the souls in Limbo (*Purgatorio,* Canto XXII), in contrast to Virgil's identification of her here among the soothsayers.

114 *the whole of it so thoroughly*: This passage presents additional difficulties. Eurypylus is indeed mentioned in the *Aeneid* (Book II), but the details there are very different from what Dante has Virgil claim. Calchas was the augur when the Greek fleet set sail from Aulis to lay siege to Troy. In the *Aeneid,* Eurypylus is a soldier sent to consult the oracle of Apollo to determine the most propitious time for the Greeks to sail home from Troy. (In fairness to Dante, it should be pointed out that Calchas does figure briefly in this incident also.)

116 *was Michael Scot*: Michael Scot (c. 1175–c. 1235), so called because of his national origin, was a philosopher and astrologer at the court of Frederick II (see note to Canto X, line 119) at Palermo. He wrote a number of works dealing with the occult sciences and translated Arabic versions of Aristotle into Latin.

118 *See Guido Bonatti. Asdente*: Benvenuto, called Asdente ("toothless"), was a shoemaker from Parma who was said to possess magical powers. The astrologer and soothsayer Guido Bonatti was a rooftiler from Forlì; he is believed to have been in the service of Guido da Montefeltro (see note to Canto XXVII, line 30).

125 *carrying his thornbush*: Equivalent to the man in the moon, Cain with his thornbush is above the point of demarcation between the northern hemisphere (land) and the southern (water). It is now about six in the morning.

CANTO XXI

38 *one of Saint Zita's Elders!*: Zita (d. 1270s) was a servant woman of Lucca, to whom miracles were attributed; she was known as Saint Zita, although she was not canonized until 1690. The Elders were the city's magistrates, ten in number, chosen for two-month terms. The dead soul (identified by an early commentator as Martino Bottaio, a Luccan politician who died the day on which this canto is set) is, like the others here, guilty of barratry, the buying and selling of public offices. *Evilclaws*: the name that Dante gives to the group of demons prominently featured in this canto and the following one. The word is *Malebranche* in the original.

41 *our friend Bonturo*: This line is highly ironic, since Bonturo Dati, who died in 1325, was reputed to be the most corrupt official in Lucca.

48 *no place for the Holy Face!*: An ancient crucifix in Lucca, carved from dark wood.

49 *that you did in the Serchio*: A river that flows near Lucca. According to the early commentaries, it was a popular site for swimming in summer.

95 *out of Caprona*: A castle about five miles from the city of Pisa, Caprona was surrendered to Tuscan Guelph forces (Florentines and Lucchese) in August 1289. Dante was a member of the invading army.

114 *broken by a mighty quake*: See note to Canto XII, line 45. It is now about seven o'clock on Saturday morning.

CANTO XXII

5 *seen raiding parties there*: According to a letter that has not survived, Dante was a cavalryman at the battle of Campaldino on June 11, 1289, in which the Aretine Ghibellines were defeated by the Florentine Guelphs.

21 *to keep their craft afloat*: It was believed that the surfacing of dolphins near a vessel signified an approaching storm.

48 *in the kingdom of Navarre*: Once an independent kingdom, Navarre is now divided between northern Spain and southwestern France. The speaker was named in early commentaries as one Ciampolo, but nothing is known of him.

52 *King Thibaut's retinue*: Thibaut II, king of Navarre from 1253 to 1270, was highly regarded for his justice and generosity.

81 *Fra Gomita of Gallura*: Around 1294, Fra Gomita was appointed chancellor by Nino Visconti (see note to Canto XXXIII, line 13), a Pisan who was the judge of Gallura, one of the four judicial districts of Sardinia. Visconti ignored all complaints against Gomita until he discovered that the friar had helped prisoners to escape, whereupon he had him hanged.

89 *Don Michel Zanche*: Governor of Logudoro, another of the four judicial districts of Sardinia. He was murdered by his son-in-law, Branca d'Oria (see note to Canto XXXIII, line 137).

CANTO XXIII

3 *that Friars Minor*: The Franciscans. Following the example of their founder, Saint Francis of Assisi, they cultivated poverty and humility. They made their begging rounds in pairs, the younger friar walking behind the elder.

6 *the frog and mouse*: In most versions of this fable, a mouse asks a frog to carry him across a stream; before doing so, the frog ties the mouse to his leg, and during the crossing he tries to drown the mouse by submerging; the ensuing commotion attracts a hawk, who carries them off, eating the frog and freeing the mouse.

63 *fashioned for the Cluny monks*: The abbey of Cluny in Burgundy was founded by the Benedictines in 910.

66–67 *Frederick would impose / seem straw*: According to his enemies (although there is no confirmation), Emperor Frederick II punished treason by having the offender boiled in a cauldron while wearing a lead cape; the cape, when it melted, peeled away the traitor's skin.

108 *in the region of the Gardingo*: The Knights of the Blessed Virgin Mary were a religious order whose charge was to reconcile factions and disputes and to protect the weak. They were known sarcastically as the Jolly Friars because of the laxity of their rules and their reputation for corruption. Among the founders of the order were Catalano di Guido di Ostia (c. 1210–1285), a Guelph, and Loderingo degli Andalò (c. 1210–1293), a Ghibelline, who served jointly as maintainers of public order in Bologna in 1265. Having arranged a truce between warring factions, they were appointed in 1266 to a similar function in Florence at the behest of Pope Clement IV, whose secret intent was to establish the Guelph party at the expense of the Ghibellines. In 1267, the Ghibellines were driven out of Florence, their property confiscated, and the houses of some of the more prominent families destroyed, including those of the Uberti family in the Gardingo section of the city.

124 *so much evil for the Jews*: Caiaphas, the high priest of the Jews, urged that Jesus be turned over to the Romans, ostensibly for the public good but secretly because Jesus's teachings posed a threat to the established leadership. In this he was abetted by his father-in-law, Annas, and other members of the Sanhedrin, the supreme council. From this betrayal, as Dante sees it, followed the destruction of Jerusalem and the diaspora.

CANTO XXIV

3 *equaling the days*: The sun is in Aquarius between January 21 and February 21.

88 *the Red Sea's lands*: Libya (the ancient term for northern Africa, exclusive of Egypt), Ethiopia (from Egypt south to Zanzibar), and Arabia ("the Red Sea's lands") were considered to be largely uninhabitable and filled with exotic creatures. All the species of serpents mentioned here are taken from Book IX of Lucan's *Pharsalia*.

125 *I am Vanni Fucci*: Vanni Fucci was the illegitimate son ("mule") of Fuccio dei Lazzari and an extreme partisan of the Blacks in Pistoia. He was notorious for his rage and was known to have committed at least one murder (thus Dante's surprise, in lines 128–29, at finding him here and not among the violent).

139 *blamed for what I'd done*: The theft of sacred objects from the sacristy of the chapel of San Jacopo caused a sensation in Pistoia in 1293. Fucci revealed his involvement in this crime in order to save the life of one Rampino di Francesco Foresi, who was about to be hanged for it.

151 *to give you pain*: Fucci's prophecy alludes to the following events: In May 1301, the Pistoian Whites, with the aid of their Florentine counterparts, expelled the Blacks from their city. In November of that year, the Blacks began an uprising in Florence that led to their recapture of the city the following year and the banishment of the Whites, which would result in Dante's permanent exile from Florence (see note to Canto VI, line 75). The "vapor"—or hot wind, which clashes with the cold, moist clouds to produce the storm—is generally understood to be Moroello Malaspina, from the region of Val di Magra, a highly effective military leader of the Blacks. Campo Piceno refers to a field near Pistoia, believed to be the site of Catiline's defeat in 63 B.C.E., and also the location of a raid by Malaspina against the Whites.

CANTO XXV

12 *surpass your seed in villainy?*: The "seed" of Pistoia was presumed to be the remains of the defeated army of Catiline; see note to Canto XV, line 78, for similar presumptions regarding the origins of Florence.

15 *fell from the high wall*: The reference is to Capaneus (see Canto XIV, lines 43–72).

19 *not even Maremma*: The Maremma (see note to Canto XIII, line 8) was, in addition to its other harsh features, swampy and snake-infested.

25 *That centaur there is Cacus*: Son of Vulcan and Medusa, a fire-breathing monster who lived in a cave beneath Mount Avetine and preyed upon travelers. In Book VIII of the *Aeneid*, Virgil describes him as "half-human"; Dante has adapted these details to make him a centaur with a fire-breathing dragon on his back. Cacus stole some of the cattle that Hercules had taken from Geryon (see note to Canto XVII, line 1), for which he was slain by Hercules—strangled, according to Virgil; clubbed, according to Ovid. Other centaurs guard the violent who are punished in the river of blood (Canto XII), but Cacus, even though he has something of a guard's function here, is punished with the thieves.

43 *to someone else—"Where's Cianfa?"*: Cianfa (d. c. 1289) appears to have been a member of the Donati family of Florence. He is the serpent who comes running up at line 50.

67–68 *and they said: / "Alas, Agnello"*: A member of the Brunelleschi family, Ghibellines of Florence. There is little historically reliable information about him.

96 *what is sent forth next*: In Book IX of *Pharsalia,* Lucan tells of Sabellus, a soldier in Cato's army who was bitten by a snake in the Libyan desert and became a festering mass, and of Nasidius, another of Cato's soldiers, also bitten by a serpent, whose body became so swollen that it burst.

98–99 *how Arethusa came to be / a fountain*: Cadmus, son of King Agenor of Phoenicia, and his wife, Harmonia, were turned into serpents for killing a dragon sacred to Mars (*Metamorphoses,* Book IV), and the nymph Arethusa was transformed into a fountain to escape the river god Alpheus, who nonetheless mingled his waters with hers (Book V).

140 *Now I'll let Buoso*: Variously identified, Buoso is believed to have been Buoso di Forese Donati (d. c. 1285; not the Buoso Donati mentioned in Canto XXX, line 43).

147–148 *I could clearly recognize / Puccio Sciancato*: Puccio Galigai, called Sciancato ("lame"), was a member of a Ghibelline family and appears to have had the reputation of a gentleman thief.

151 *on whose account, Gaville*: Francesco de' Cavalcanti, called Guercio ("squinting" or "cross-eyed"), was murdered by people from Gaville, a town near Florence. The Cavalcanti avenged his death by killing many of Gaville's inhabitants. There is no solid evidence that he was a thief.

CANTO XXVI

4 *among the thieves*: The five thieves were all members of upper-class families.

7 *toward dawn are true*: There was a common belief that morning dreams are prophetic in nature.

8–9 *soon to come, / what Prato*: The reference may be either to Cardinal Niccolò da Prato, who excommunicated the city's inhabitants in 1304 after failing to reconcile its rival factions, or to the town of Prato, eleven miles northwest of the city, which expelled its Black Guelphs in 1309.

24 *it should not be misapplied*: See note to Canto IV, line 102.

39 *through the skies*: When the prophet Elisha cursed forty-two young boys who had mocked his baldness, two bears came from the forest and tore them to pieces (2 Kings 2.23–24). Elisha also beheld the prophet Elijah borne to heaven in a whirlwind by fiery horses and a fiery chariot (2 Kings 2.7–14).

54 *at his brother's side*: In the siege of Thebes (see note to Canto XIV, line 46), the warring sons of Oedipus, Eteocles and Polynices, killed one another. The dividing of the flame of their mutual pyre communicated their undying hatred.

63 *pay for the Palladium*: The condemnation of the Greek heroes Ulysses (Odysseus) and Diomedes among the fraudulent is based on three incidents, the first and third of which are drawn from Book II of the *Aeneid,* the second from the unfinished *Achilleid* of Statius: (1) They devised the Trojan horse, whose role in the fall of Troy made it the portal through which the surviving Trojans passed to become the founders of Rome. (2) They went to Scyros to lure the beardless Achilles out of hiding among the women—where his mother, the goddess Thetis, had placed him—because he would be needed for success against the Trojans; the news of his death in Troy would cause Deidamia, the mother of his son, to die of grief. (3) They sneaked into Troy by night to steal the statue of Pallas Athena, upon which the city's safety was believed to depend.

90 *and these words came*: Ulysses' speech was the primary inspiration for Tennyson's great monologue "Ulysses." It is fascinating to observe how the same material is made to yield opposite conclusions: where Dante in lines 91–142 presents Ulysses' final journey as a failure of familial responsibilities and a hubristic flouting of divinely imposed limitations, Tennyson celebrates the spirit of quest and daring without which there would be no human progress.

93 *name that beach*: Gaeta, a town on the southeastern coast of Italy, was named by Aeneas for his nurse, Caieta, who died there (*Aeneid,* Book VII). Dante would have known the story of Ulysses' entanglement with the enchantress Circe from Ovid's *Metamorphoses,* Book XIV.

111 *Ceuta already lay behind*: The narrow channel is the Strait of Gibraltar. The Pillars of Hercules are Calpe in Spain and Abyla on the African promontory. In legend, they were originally one mountain, which was torn apart by Hercules, marking the point beyond which no one may sail and survive. Seville here connotes southern Spain, near Gibraltar. Ceuta is on the north coast of Morocco opposite Gibraltar.

126 *as days flew by*: They are sailing southwest, toward the point on the globe that is exactly opposite Jerusalem, where Dante locates the Mount of Purgatory (line 134).

129 *barely was in sight*: The ship has now crossed the equator into the Southern Hemisphere.

CANTO XXVII

7 *And as the Sicilian bull*: Several classical sources tell of Phalaris, tyrant of Agrigentum in the sixth century B.C.E., who had the Athenian Perillus fashion a bronze bull in which victims would be roasted alive, with their muffled cries passing through pipes that made them sound like the bellowing of a bull. Phalaris tested the device with Perillus himself as subject.

30 *the Tiber starts its flow*: Romagna is a district in northeastern Italy stretching from the Po south to the eastern Apennines, the range that includes Mount Coronaro, where the Tiber originates. The speaker, who is never identified by name, is Guido da Montefeltro (c. 1220–1298), perhaps the greatest of the Ghibelline commanders, who kept Romagna under Ghibelline rule when most of

Italy, including the papacy, was Guelph-dominated. The bane of several popes, he was excommunicated in 1289, but was later reconciled to the church and joined the Franciscan order (the "corded friars" of lines 67–68) in 1296.

42 *his wings are spread*: Guido da Polenta, whose coat of arms displayed an eagle, had ruled Ravenna since 1275. Cervia is a town on the Adriatic, southeast of Ravenna. Guido was the father of Francesca da Rimini (see note to Canto V, line 97) and the grandfather of Guido Novello, who was Dante's host in Ravenna in 1321.

45 *the green paws once again*: Forlì, the central city of Romagna, held off a year-long siege by a Guelph army, of French and Italian troops, sent by Pope Martin IV. The successful defense of the city was directed by Guido da Montefeltro, whom Dante does not yet realize he is addressing. "Green paws" alludes to the escutcheon of the Ordelaffi family, who despotically ruled Forlì at the end of the thirteenth century.

48 *as they are wont to do*: In 1295, when the Ghibellines of Rimini were defeated by Malatesta da Verrucchio, the Ghibelline leader, Montagna de' Parcitati, was captured and then killed by Malatesta's son Malatestino. Malatesta ruled until his death in 1312, at the age of one hundred, when he was succeeded by Malatestino, who was succeeded in 1317 by his brother Pandolfo. Malatesta's other sons were Gianciotto, the husband of Francesca da Rimini, and Paolo, her lover.

51 *he turns his coat*: Faenza is on the river Lamone, Imola on the Santerno. In 1300, they were under the control of Maghinardo de' Pagani da Susinana, here called the "lionet" because of his coat of arms. He was known for his political inconsistency.

54 *between the plain and mountain*: Cesena was ruled by the relatively benign Galasso da Montefeltro, Guido's cousin.

66 *without fear of infamy*: Lines 61–66, untranslated and unidentified, were used by T. S. Eliot as the epigraph to "The Love Song of J. Alfred Prufrock."

70 *may his spirit rot in hell*: The corrupt pope alluded to here is Boniface VIII.

90 *the sultan's will is done*: There was endless strife, erupting into armed conflict in 1297, between Boniface and the powerful Colonna family, whose residences were not far from his own, the Lateran Palace. The Colonna refused to accept the abdication of Celestine V (see note to Canto III, line 60) and thus denied the legitimacy of Boniface's papacy. Here Boniface is attacked for launching a crusade against his fellow Christians, while doing nothing to oppose the Saracens who in 1291 had conquered Acre, the last Christian stronghold in the Holy Land, or to punish those who defied the order, imposed by Pope Nicholas IV after the fall of Acre, forbidding all commerce with Muslim lands.

93 *thin in times before*: The cord worn by the Franciscan friars made its wearers thin through their adherence to the vows of poverty and abstinence; "in times before" is an attack on the corruption of the contemporary church.

95 *to cure his leprosy*: It was widely believed during the Middle Ages that Constantine, afflicted with leprosy for his persecution of Christians, sent for Pope

Sylvester I, who was hiding in a cave on Mount Soracte; Constantine was cured instantly upon being baptized by Sylvester and, according to the fraudulent Donation of Constantine, gave the church temporal power in the western part of the empire (see note to Canto XIX, line 118).

102 *how I may cause Penestrino's demolition*: Palestrina (Praeneste in ancient times) is a city some twenty miles east of Rome, where the Colonna resisted Boniface's siege until September 1298, when they surrendered under promise of amnesty. Supposedly, although their lives were spared, the Colonna were ruined and the city was destroyed.

111 *keeping short and small*: It is not clear whether Guido actually gave Boniface such advice, since later chroniclers may have had Dante as their only source for the story.

112 *when I died*: According to Singleton, "The transition is the more effective for being so abrupt. Guido in fact did die in September 1298, the month in which Boniface tricked the Colonna."

CANTO XXVIII

7 *Apulia's battle dead*: Puglia is the southeastern corner of Italy, the heel of the boot. Dante uses the term, as was common in his time, to denote the entire southern portion of the peninsula. He alludes to several battles, ancient and modern, that were fought there, beginning with the invasion by Aeneas and his forces.

12 *what he tells is true*: According to Livy (Titus Livius, 59 B.C.E.–17 C.E.) in his monumental history of Rome, *Ab urbe condita,* Hannibal had his soldiers remove the rings of Roman officers they had killed at the battle of Cannae (216 B.C.E.), an Apulian village, and sent them to the Carthaginian senate to demonstrate the magnitude of his victory. The "long war" was the Second Punic War (218–201 B.C.E.).

14 *resisted Robert Guiscard's*: Robert Guiscard (1015–1085), brother of the duke of Normandy, was made ruler of Apulia and Calabria by Pope Nicholas II. He spent twenty years battling the Greeks and Saracens in southern Italy, and is cited in Canto XVIII of the *Paradiso* among warriors for the faith.

16 *failed by Apulian faithlessness*: The forces of King Manfred of Sicily met the invading army of Charles of Anjou near Benevento (not Ceprano) on February 26, 1266. When his Apulian allies fled the field, Manfred chose to die in battle rather than flee. Because he had been excommunicated, he was buried in unconsecrated ground and subsequently disinterred (according to some, on the orders of Pope Clement IV). In Canto III of the *Purgatorio*, Manfred is the first penitent soul Dante encounters as he begins his ascent of the mountain.

18 *won the victory weaponless*: In 1268, Charles of Anjou fought Conradin, nephew of Manfred and grandson of Frederick II, near Tagliacozzo. Charles was advised by the chevalier Érard de Valéry (c. 1200–c. 1277) to hold back his reserves as long as possible, which strategy turned the tide of battle in his favor.

31 *see mangled Mohammed tear himself!*: Ronald L. Martinez and Robert M. Durling state: "In the Christian polemics that were Dante's sources of information, Mohammed was said to have been a Nestorian Christian (the Nestorians denied that Christ's divine and human natures were united) before founding Islam; thus he was thought both a heretic and a schismatic, having drawn one third of the world's believers away from the true faith" (*The* Divine Comedy *of Dante Alighieri. Volume I:* Inferno, Oxford, 1996). According to Mark Musa, Dante's treatment of Mohammed "reflects the medieval belief that Mohammed was responsible not only for a schism but the invasion of Palestine and the dismantling of Christian power and influence in the Middle East. Opinion in Dante's day ignored the fact that Mohammed was a monotheist in a pagan culture and that his split from Christianity followed the development of its trinitarian dogma."

32 *and weeping is Ali*: Ali (c. 592–661) was Mohammed's cousin and son-in-law. Controversy over his assumption of the caliphate in 656 led to the splitting of Islam into the Sunni and Shiite sects.

60 *find difficult to achieve*: Dolcino Tornielli of Novara was known as Fra Dolcino because of his association with the Apostolic Brethren, who sought to bring the church back to the simplicity of its earliest times, the days of the Apostles. After the death of the group's founder, Gherardo Segarelli, Dolcino took command of the Brethren. He was accused of holding heretical views, and in 1305 Pope Clement V preached against the sect. Dolcino and a large group of his followers, including his companion and presumed mistress, Margaret of Trent, held out for some time in the hills between Novara and Vercelli, but were driven out by hunger and repeated attacks. Dolcino and Margaret were captured in June 1307 and burned at the stake.

75 *keep Pier da Medicina*: Medicina is a town between Bologna and Imola. Pier has not been positively identified. The "sweet plain" is the entire Po valley.

90 *Focara's perilous wind be pacified*: The incident in question, for which there is no definite historical authority, is believed to have occurred around 1312. Guido del Cassero and Angiolello di Carignano were leaders of opposing political parties in Fano. La Cattolica is midway between Fano and Rimini on the Adriatic coast. The references to Cyprus and Majorca signify the entire extent of the Mediterranean; the Argives are the people of Argos—broadly speaking, the Greeks. The "one-eyed traitor" is Malatestino, ruler of Rimini (see note to Canto XXVII, line 48).

102 *whose speech had always dared*: Gaius Scribonius Curio the Younger was a follower of Pompey, then went over to Julius Caesar, and in the ensuing civil war led the campaign that drove Cato's army out of Sicily. Dante follows Lucan in claiming that it was on the advice of Curio that Caesar decided to cross the Rubicon at Rimini, which action marked the beginning of the civil war.

109 *killed off your whole line*: In 1215, Buondelmonte de' Buondelmonti, a Florentine noble, broke his engagement to a daughter of the Amidei for what he considered a better offer. When allies of the Amidei discussed how best to avenge the shame, Mosca dei Lamberti spoke the words signifying that the matter should be resolved with finality, by the death of Buondelmonte, and himself took part in the murder. Although there had previously been tension between the Guelphs and Ghibellines, this killing crystallized the hostility that was to plague the city thereafter. Dante's taunt in line 109 refers to the expulsion of the Lamberti from Florence in 1258, after which they no longer figured in the affairs of the city. In Canto VI, line 80, Dante had asked Ciacco about Mosca's posthumous whereabouts.

136 *the father fought the son*: Bertran de Born (c. 1140–c. 1215) was one of the greatest of the Provençal troubadours. Ezra Pound adapted or loosely translated several of his poems, including the "Planh for the Young English King," Bertran's elegy for Prince Henry (1155–1183), second and oldest surviving son of King Henry II and called "the young king" because he was twice crowned during his father's lifetime. Encouraged by his mother, Eleanor of Aquitaine, and King Louis VII of France, Prince Henry rebelled against his father, demanding that he be given a substantial portion of his patrimony. The ensuing conflict lasted until "the young king" died of a fever; unlike his younger brothers, Richard and John, he never attained the throne.

138 *with King David and Absalon*: In 2 Samuel 15–17, Ahithophel counseled Absalom to rebel against his father, King David, a course of action that led to Absalom's death and Ahithophel's suicide.

142 *retribution takes its course*: This line is the poem's only direct mention of the *contrapasso*, the principle of fitting the punishment to the nature of the offense.

CANTO XXIX

27 *called Geri del Bello*: Geri del Bello degli Alighieri was a first cousin of Dante's father. According to Dante's son Pietro, he was murdered by Brodaio dei Sacchetti, a murder that was not avenged until many years later, in 1310. Peace between the feuding families was not arranged until 1342. Vengeance for the murders of one's kinsmen was sanctioned by both law and custom.

29 *that once held Hautefort*: The castle of Bertran de Born.

48 *and Valdichiana's too*: Like the island of Sardinia, the Tuscan areas of the Maremma (see notes to Canto XIII, line 8, and Canto XXV, line 19) and the Valdichiana are swampy, and in medieval times all were breeding grounds for malaria in the summer.

64 *sprang into life again*: As the story is told in Book VII of Ovid's *Metamorphoses*, Aeacus was the son of Jupiter (Zeus) and the nymph Aegina, and ruler of the island that bore his mother's name. After Juno (Hera) devastated the island with a plague, Zeus repopulated it by turning its ants into men (hence the name Myrmidons for the inhabitants, from the Greek for "ant"). Aeacus was the father of Peleus and the grandfather of Achilles.

110 *at Albero of Siena's will*: Early commentators identify the Aretine as one Griffolino, who was burned at the stake for heresy around 1272. The credulous Albero was the protégé and perhaps the actual son of the bishop of Siena.

132 *showed his wit*: Stricca, about whom nothing is known for certain, has been tentatively identified with Stricca di Giovanni de' Salimbeni, whose brother Niccolò was a member of the *brigata spendereccia* ("spendthrifts' club"), a group of young Sienese nobles who dedicated themselves to squandering their wealth as lavishly as possible, and were believed to have run through their entire fortunes in less than two years. Some claim that Niccolò introduced cloves, then extremely expensive, to the "garden" of Siena. Other spendthrifts in good standing were Caccia d'Asciano and Bartolommeo dei Folcacchieri, called Abbagliato, or "bedazzled." Meo was fined in 1278 for drinking in a tavern.

136 *I am Capocchio's shade*: Capocchio was burned alive at Siena in 1293. Some early commentators claim that he and Dante knew one another as students.

CANTO XXX

12 *her other charge and drowned*: Semele was the daughter of Cadmus, founder of Thebes, and one of the many loves of Zeus. After Semele was accidentally killed by lightning when Zeus manifested himself to her in his godly form, their unborn child was saved, placed in Zeus's thigh and ultimately born there, and then given to Semele's sister, Ino. Her wrath unabated, Hera maddened Athamas, Ino's husband, making him kill their son Learchus; Ino then leaped into the sea with their other son, Melicertes (Ovid, *Metamorphoses*, Book IV).

21 *had so wrenched her mind*: Hecuba, widow of King Priam of Troy, and her daughter Polyxena were enslaved by the conquering Greeks. Hecuba was driven mad by the sacrifice of Polyxena on the tomb of Achilles and her discovery of the body of her murdered son Polydorus, which had washed up on the shore.

31 *That lunatic is Gianni Schicchi*: According to early commentators, after Buoso Donati died intestate, his nephew Simone enlisted Gianni Schicchi (d. c. 1280), of the Cavalcanti family, to impersonate the dead man and dictate a will in Simone's favor. During the impersonation, Schicchi proceeded to make lavish bequests to himself of Donati's property. The story is the basis of Giacomo Puccini's one-act opera, one of the components of his *Trittico*.

39 *beyond the bounds of all propriety*: For her refusal to honor the goddess Aphrodite, Myrrha was afflicted with an incestuous passion for her father, King Cinyras of Cyprus. After she seduced him by impersonating her mother, he threatened to kill her. She fled, and was turned into a myrtle (or myrrh) tree, from whose trunk Adonis was born (Ovid, *Metamorphoses*, Book X).

60–61 *take note / of Master Adam*: A Master Adam, an Englishman, was identified in a 1277 document as a member of the household of the Conti Guidi of Romena, a village in the region of the Casentino, east of Florence. In 1281, someone in their employ was burned alive for coining florins with twenty-one carats of gold instead of twenty-four; the first gold florin had been coined in 1252, and soon became the standard gold coin throughout Europe. The Guidi were four brothers in all; the two not named in line 77 were Aghinolfo and Ildebrandino. The reference in line 80 must be to Guido, who also died in 1281; the other three were still alive in 1300. There is a Fonte Branda in Romena and a more famous one in Siena; it is not clear which one is meant.

97 *Joseph's accuser is that lying wench*: The wife of Potiphar, an officer of Pharaoh, made repeated attempts to seduce Joseph, who was her husband's overseer. Spurned by him, she made the false accusation that he had tried to assault her sexually, and he was imprisoned (Genesis 39.6–20).

98 *Sinon, Troy's false Greek*: Sinon allowed himself to be captured by the Trojans, claiming falsely that he had escaped his fate as an intended sacrifice by the Greeks and that the Trojan horse was meant as an atonement to Athena for the theft of the Palladium (see note to Canto XXVI, line 63). On the basis of his lies, the Trojans took the horse into the city.

129 *the mirror of Narcissus a good lick*: The reference is to a surface of water, like that of the fountain in which the beautiful youth Narcissus became enamored of his own image, ultimately dying of despair over his inability to possess it.

CANTO XXXI

6 *then a good one in its stead*: The spear of Achilles had the power to heal the wounds that it inflicted. Homer asserts that the spear had previously belonged to Achilles' father, Peleus. But Dante, who did not know Greek, seems, like other medieval poets, to have made this association through a misreading of Ovid, mistaking a reference to Mount Pelion for an allusion to Peleus.

16 *blew so fiercely*: As recounted in the *Chanson de Roland,* Ganelon, the stepfather of Roland, betrayed the rear guard of Charlemagne's army to the Saracens at Roncesvalles in 778. Roland blew his horn to summon the main force to their rescue, but Ganelon dissuaded Charlemagne from responding, and Roland and all his companions were killed.

40 *For just as Montereggione*: A heavily fortified castle outside Siena. Fourteen towers, each over sixty feet tall, were added to its walls after the battle of Montaperti (see note to Canto X, line 32).

43 *thunders from on high*: Jove still thunders because of the giants' assault on Mount Olympus (see Canto XIV, lines 52–60, and note to line 58).

59 *on the holy ground*: The bronze pinecone, now located in the Belvedere Gardens of the papal palace, is about thirteen feet high.

63 *so that three Frieslanders*: Frieslanders, or Frisians, inhabitants of the Frisian Islands in the North Sea, were known for their great height.

65 *for I noted thirty spans*: A span is the width of an outstretched hand, roughly nine inches.

67 *"Raphèl maì amècche zabì almi!" tore*: A number of attempts have been made
   to decipher Nimrod's words, despite the clear indication in lines 80–81 that
   they are unintelligible.

78 *not one common language everywhere*: Nimrod, king of Babylon, is described
   in Genesis 10.9 as "a mighty hunter before the Lord," which may account for
   his horn. According to tradition, it was he who built the tower of Babel.

94 *struck the great blows*: In an attempt to scale the heavens during the assault on
   the gods, Ephialtes and his brother Otus tried to pile Ossa on Olympus and
   Pelion on Ossa, but were killed by Zeus.

99 *Briareus in his immensity*: Briareus is another of the giants who made war on
   Olympus. In the *Aeneid*, he is described as fifty-headed and hundred-handed.
   By deflecting Dante from viewing him and by characterizing him as normally
   shaped, Virgil seems to implicitly acknowledge the absurdity of that depiction.

100 *You will see Antaeus*: The son of Neptune and Gaea (Earth), who retained his
   great strength by maintaining contact with his mother. He wrestled Hercules
   (lines 131–32), who lifted him off the ground and crushed him to death. His
   unfettered state may be a result of his not participating in the assault on Olym-
   pus, which took place before he was born.

117 *his army turned around*: Scipio defeated Hannibal at Zama in North Africa in
   202 B.C.E., resolving the Second Punic War in favor of Rome.

123 *in which Cocytus*: The frozen lake of the ninth circle of hell; in Cocytus are
   embedded the worst of all sinners.

125 *to Tityus or Typhon*: Typhon, who had a hundred fire-breathing serpent
   heads, was killed by the thunderbolts of Zeus. Tityus was a giant killed by
   Apollo and Artemis when he attempted to rape their mother, Leto.

136 *As the Garisenda*: Built around 1110, the Garisenda, is the smaller of two
   leaning towers in Bologna.

CANTO XXXII

11 *that inspired Amphion*: The Muses helped Amphion wall Thebes by inspiring
   him to play so beautifully upon the lyre that the stones came down from
   Mount Cithaeron to form the walls themselves.

29 *of Tambernic or Pietrapana*: Mount Pietrapana is in the Apuan Alps; Tamber-
   nic is most likely Mount Tambura, in the same range.

56 *was their father's*: Alessandro and Napoleone were the sons of Count Alberto
   of Mangona. According to the early commentators, they fought over their
   inheritance and wound up killing one another sometime in the 1280s.

62 *not Focaccia*: The nickname of Vanni de' Cancellieri, who murdered his cousin
   Detto di Sinibaldo Cancellieri in 1293. "Arthur": King Arthur was killed by
   Mordred, his treacherous nephew (or son). In their mutually fatal encounter,
   Arthur pierced him through with his lance, inflicting so gaping a wound that a
   ray of light passed through Mordred's body.

64 *who was Sassol Mascheroni*: He murdered one of his relatives over an inheritance. In punishment for the crime, he was rolled through the streets of Florence in a nail-filled cask and then beheaded.

68 *was Camiscion de' Pazzi*: Of Alberto Camicione de' Pazzi of Val d'Arno, all that is known for certain is that he murdered a relative named Ubertino. In 1302, Carlino de' Pazzi, another kinsman of his, would accept a bribe to betray the castle of Piantravigne to the Black Guelphs. Camicione's guilt will be mitigated because his cousin's treachery will be of a more serious kind than his own and qualify him for the next zone, Antenora (named for Antenor, who in Dante's time was believed to have betrayed Troy to the Greeks).

81 *revenge for Montaperti*: At the battle of Montaperti in 1260 (see note to Canto X, line 32), Bocca degli Abati, a Ghibelline infiltrator, cut off the hand of the Guelph standard-bearer, creating a panic that led to a crushing defeat for the Guelphs.

116 *the one from Duera*: Buoso da Duera of Cremona, a Ghibelline leader, was allegedly bribed by the French in 1265 to allow the forces of Charles of Anjou to pass unresisted through Lombardy on their way to Naples to attack Manfred (see note to Canto XXVIII, line 16).

119 *right by your side's a Beccheria*: Tesauro de' Beccheria was abbot of Vallombrosa and papal legate of Alexander IV. After the Ghibellines were expelled from Florence in 1258, he was accused of conspiring with them, and was subsequently tortured and beheaded.

121 *Gianni de' Soldanieri and Ganelon*: For Ganelon, see note to Canto XXXI, line 16. When the Florentines rebelled against their Ghibelline rulers in 1266, Gianni de' Soldanieri deserted his party and joined the Guelphs in an unsuccessful attempt to advance himself politically.

122 *are further along. Tebaldello*: Tebaldello belonged to the Zambrasi, a Ghibelline family of Faenza. Because of personal hostility to members of the Lambertazzi, Ghibelline exiles from Bologna who had taken refuge in Faenza, he opened the gates of the city to their Guelph enemies in the predawn hours of November 13, 1280.

130 *Not even Tydeus*: Tydeus, one of the seven kings besieging Thebes (see note to Canto XIV, line 46), exchanged fatal blows with the Theban Menalippus. According to Statius, the dying Tydeus called for the head of Menalippus and proceeded to gnaw it in his rage.

CANTO XXXIII

12–13 *my name / was Count Ugolino*: Ugolino della Gherardesca, Conte di Donoratico (c. 1220–1289), belonged to a noble Ghibelline family of Pisa. He was banished after the failure of his intrigue with the Guelph leader Giovanni Visconti in 1275, but returned to Pisa the following year and quickly reassumed a position of power. He conspired with the archbishop, Ruggieri degli Ubaldini, also a Ghibelline, to rid the city of Nino Visconti, who was a judge, a Guelph, Ugolino's grandson, and a friend of Dante's. After they had driven Visconti out of Pisa in 1288, Ruggieri turned on Ugolino, accusing him of betraying the city because he had, in 1285, ceded castles to Florence and to Lucca. Whether Ugolino's action was intended to betray Pisa or to preserve it by conciliating its powerful foes is open to question. In any event, he was imprisoned in the summer of 1288 with two sons and two grandsons, the youngest of whom was fifteen (not the four young sons that Dante gives him). All five were starved to death early in 1289.

23 *in memory of my plight*: The Torre della Fame, or "Tower of Hunger," was used as a prison until 1318.

30 *that blocks Lucca from the view*: Monte San Giuliano stands between Pisa and Lucca.

32–33 *and that other one, / Lanfranchi*: The Gualandi, Sismondi, and Lanfranchi were prominent Ghibelline families of Pisa who supported Ruggieri in his actions against Ugolino.

82 *let Capraia and Gorgona*: Capraia and Gorgona are Mediterranean islands then belonging to Pisa.

87–88 *upon the cross that way. / New Thebes*: Thebes had a reputation as the worst city of the ancient world for violence and bloodshed.

118 *I am Fra Alberigo*: A member of the Manfredi family of Faenza and of the Jolly Friars (see note to Canto XXIII, line 108). A close relative of his named Manfred struck him in the course of an argument over the lordship of Faenza. Alberigo pretended to forgive the insult. In 1285, he invited Manfred and one of his sons to dinner. His calling to his servants to bring in the fruit was a signal for assassins to rush into the room and kill Manfred and his son. The comment made by Alberigo (who was still alive in 1300) at line 120 turns on the fact that dates were more expensive than figs.

125 *such is Ptolomea's*: The third of the four zones of Cocytus, named either for Ptolemy XII, king of Egypt, who allowed his guest, Pompey, to be murdered, or for the Ptolemy who killed Simon the Maccabee and two of his sons at a banquet (1 Maccabees 16.11–16).

126 *has yet to cut its thread*: The Fates, described by Hesiod as daughters of the night, are represented as spinning women: Clotho winds the yarn on the distaff of Lachesis, and Atropos cuts the thread of life.

137 *He is Ser Branca d'Oria*: A member of a Ghibelline family of Genoa who murdered his father-in-law, Don Michel Zanche (see note to Canto XXII, line 89) at a banquet to which he had invited him. Branca (who lived until at least 1325) was assisted in the murder by one of his relatives, either a cousin or a nephew.

CANTO XXXIV

1 Vexila regis prodeunt inferni: "Vexila regis prodeunt" ("The banners of the King advance") is the first line of a Latin hymn written in 569 by Venantius Fortunatus, bishop of Poitiers.

46 *spread out below each face*: Satan, or Lucifer, had belonged to the angelic order of the Seraphim: "In the year that King Uzziah died I saw also the Lord sitting upon a throne, high and lifted up, and his train filled the temple. Above it stood the seraphims: each one had six wings; with twain he covered his face, and with twain he covered his feet, and with twain he did fly" (Isaiah 6.1–2).

94 *The sun returns now to mid-tierce*: Tierce is the first of four three-hour periods of the day (6:00 to 9:00 A.M.). Virgil had said in line 68 that the night was rising, but it is now about 7:30 A.M., since he and Dante have crossed the earth's midpoint and are now in the Southern Hemisphere, where it is day when it is night on the other, inhabited side of the world.

124–125 *may have fled, / rushing upward*: The earth's interior, which rushed upward to avoid the fall of Satan, then formed the Mount of Purgatory. These lines thus create a transition to the *Purgatorio*.

127 *As far from Beelzebub*: Although others see them as separate devils, Dante uses the name Beelzebub here to refer to Satan.

139 *we came outside and saw the stars*: The journey to the surface, encapsulated in the previous two tercets, has taken nearly twenty-four hours. In this concluding line, Virgil and Dante emerge to see the dawn sky. "Stars" (*stelle*) will also be the last word of each of the other two parts of the *Comedy*.

ABOUT THE NORTON LIBRARY

Exciting texts you can't get anywhere else

The Norton Library is the only series that offers an inexpensive, student-friendly edition of Emily Wilson's groundbreaking version of Homer's *Odyssey*, or Carole Satyamurti's thrilling, prize-winning rendition of the *Mahabharata*, or Michael Palma's virtuoso *terza rima* translation of Dante's *Inferno*—to name just three of its unique offerings. Distinctive translations like these, exclusive to the Norton Library, are the cornerstone of the list, but even texts originally written in English offer unique distinctions. Where else, for instance, will you find an edition of John Stuart Mill's *Utilitarianism* edited and introduced by Peter Singer? Only in the Norton Library.

The Norton touch

For more than 75 years, W. W. Norton has published texts that are edited with the needs of students in mind. Volumes in the Norton Library all offer editorial features that help students read with more understanding and pleasure—to encounter the world of the work on its own terms, but also to have a trusted travel guide navigate them through that world's unfamiliar territory.

Easy to afford, a pleasure to own

Volumes in the Norton Library are inexpensive—among the most affordable texts available—but they are designed and produced with great care to be easy on the eyes, comfortable in the hand, and a pleasure to read and re-read over a lifetime.

W. W. NORTON & COMPANY
Independent Publishers Since 1923